ETHEL PERCY ANDRUS

ONE WOMAN WHO CHANGED AMERICA

BY CRAIG WALKER

CONTENTS

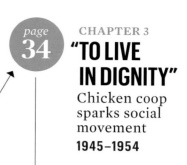

"That is the challenge: to live up to our better selves, to believe well of our fellow men, and perhaps by so doing, to help create the good we believe in."

—ETHEL PERCY ANDRUS

FOREWORD

AFTER FINDING an older woman living in a chicken coop because she could not afford decent housing or health care, a retired educator named Ethel Percy Andrus got angry, then got organized. And in doing so, she radically changed the landscape of America.

Dr. Andrus' passion for making things better flowed from her tenure as an idealistic young teacher in Chicago in the early 1900s, serving struggling immigrant families seeking their American dreams. Later, as the longtime principal of Lincoln High School in a multiethnic neighborhood of Los Angeles, she inspired her students to seize their opportunities.

After retiring in 1944 from the career she loved to nurse her mother back to health, Dr. Andrus soon realized that older people needed her as much as her students once had.

At that time, older people were seen as a societal problem. Dr. Andrus saw them as a solution—an enormous reservoir of talent and experience just waiting to be tapped.

She established two organizations—the National Retired Teachers Association and, later, the American Association of Retired Persons (now AARP)—to foster independence, dignity and purpose among people as they age.

As a social innovator, she pioneered marketplace solutions to help older Americans stretch their dollars and improve the quality of their lives, such as affordable group health insurance, a discount drug-buying plan and a travel service.

As a practical idealist, she dreamed big and worked hard to prevent juvenile delinquency, create affordable housing for people as they age and unite the generations through volunteerism.

As a useful citizen, she promoted patriotism, civic engagement and unity amidst an increasingly diverse population.

And as a devoted educator, early in her career she shaped young minds as a high school principal by day and adult minds during innovative evening classes. Later, she founded the Institute of Lifetime Learning to satisfy older adults' endless curiosity.

When asked the secret behind her extraordinary stamina, the then 81-year-old dynamo quipped, "I had a redheaded mother and a father who had a red beard. Perhaps this accounts for my fireball proclivities."

She worked diligently to make life better for others until she died, leaving few personal notes or photos but a profound legacy of historic writings and achievements.

This is her story.

Craig Walker, author
Historian and educator
Curator, Ojai Valley Museum
exhibit on Ethel Percy Andrus

CHAPTER 1

"THE URGE TO

Ethel Percy Andrus with her mother, Lucretia

Andrus was born in bustling San Francisco, with its cable cars and flourishing neighborhoods.

SERVE"

Nurturing a passion to lead

S AN FRANCISCO, in 1881, was booming. Cable cars were running on Nob Hill. New neighborhoods were blooming. The city's population had quadrupled in the past 20 years. Into that scene, on September 21, Ethel Percy Andrus was born. Her life would come to reflect—and embrace—the vibrancy, excitement and possibilities surrounding her.

Ethel's ancestors had adventure in their blood. Her mother's father was an English ship captain who sailed into San Francisco Bay, only to find that gold had just been discovered in California. The crew evidently deserted him to try their luck as prospectors. He never returned to sea.

Ethel's father, George Wallace Andrus, was an aspiring lawyer from upstate New York. He traveled west to San Francisco, where he met Ethel's mother, Lucretia Frances Duke.

George and Lucretia were married and soon had two girls: Maud, followed by Ethel. To support his young family, George worked as a barber and later ran a furniture business.

"My parents were young folk, eager, dedicated and very, very human," Ethel would recall.

Her father was a public-spirited man who believed in giving back to the community. Ethel would follow his example throughout her life.

Ethel attended the Mission Primary School, where the principal, Mrs. M.H. Walker, was an early female role model. By the 1880s most public-school teachers were women—education was one of the few professions open to females—but men still dominated the ranks of school administrators.

The Chicago of Ethel's childhood, teeming with industry and immigration

Growing Up in Chicago

EORGE ANDRUS MOVED his family to Chicago in 1890 so he could complete his law studies at Northwestern University. He earned his degree and passed the Illinois bar exam in 1892 and began practicing law in Chicago. Ethel later remembered her father as "a struggling young attorney" and her mother as "his proud and admiring helpmate." The parents instilled in their two daughters a progressive spirit, a love of learning and a determination to make the most of their opportunities.

After the move, Ethel resumed her studies at a school on the South Side of Chicago. When she was 11, the world suddenly beat a path to her door, or so it must have seemed. Millions of people flocked to the South Side in the summer of 1893 and were dazzled by Chicago's World's Fair, which showcased the nation's technical, cultural and artistic achievements. Formally titled the World's Columbian Exposition, the fair introduced America to such enduring phenomena as Cracker Jack and the Ferris wheel. From the wheel's peak, Ethel would have enjoyed a splendid view of the fair's White City, an impressive complex of neoclassical buildings—constructed out of plaster and wood and painted white to resemble marble—designed by the nation's most prominent architects.

"Make no little plans," lead architect Daniel Burnham was often quoted as saying. "They have no magic to stir men's blood and probably themselves will not be realized. Make big plans; aim high in hope and work, re-membering that a noble, logical diagram once recorded will never die, but long after we are gone will be a living thing, asserting itself with ever-growing insistency. Remember that our sons and our grandsons are going to do things that would stagger us."

Our daughters and granddaughters, too. Four decades later, when Ethel Percy Andrus founded the National Retired Teachers Association "on a shoestring and a prayer," she echoed Burnham's words.

"We made no little plans," she would write, "for in little plans lies no magic to stir one's blood. We made big plans. We aimed high in hope and work. We counted upon our people's determination and their missionary spirit. We did not count in vain."

> ## "My parents were young folk, eager, dedicated and very, very human."
> *—Ethel Percy Andrus*

Ethel with her older sister, Maud

George Andrus

"Make no little plans; they have no magic to stir men's blood."

—DANIEL BURNHAM

architect, 1893 Chicago World's Fair

THE SOUTH SIDE was also the epicenter of the violent Pullman Strike of 1894. A sudden financial panic had plunged the nation into a deep depression, igniting an acrimonious dispute between Chicago railroad workers and their employers. President Grover Cleveland sent in federal troops to restore order. His soldiers crushed the strike, along with the enthusiastic spirit from the recent World's Fair. The strike fueled bitter class conflict, which greatly disturbed upper-class reformers like Jane Addams. She believed strongly in the power of negotiation and arbitration. Antagonism, she told John Dewey, a philosophy professor at the University of Chicago, "was not only useless and harmful but entirely unnecessary." He was impressed by her arguments—and so, it seems, was Ethel Andrus, who throughout her life as an activist favored negotiation over confrontation.

Chicago surely influenced Ethel emotionally and intellectually. All of America's contradictions, its glories and its agonies, were on display. She grew up to be a proudly patriotic American, determined to help her country live up to its high ideals.

In the late 1800s, most girls modeled themselves on plucky fictional heroines such as Jane Eyre or Jo from *Little Women*. Others admired first lady Frances Cleveland, President Cleveland's beautiful wife. Ethel was different. Her idol was the late Peter Cooper, a wealthy industrialist and inventor turned philanthropist who founded the Cooper Union for the Advancement of Science and Art, a New York college that offered free night classes to all comers, regardless of their sex, race or socioeconomic background.

"One of my earliest memories is the great impression made upon me by the story of Peter Cooper and his love for, and service to, folks whom he might never have known," Ethel would later say. "I wanted, above everything else, to be like him. Perhaps this urge to serve was

Pullman Strike of 1894

BITTER CLASS CONFLICT

They called it the Gilded Age: millionaires building mansions while poor people piled into teeming tenements; newfangled skyscrapers towering over dark, oppressive mills; a boom-and-bust economy that powered the nation to giddy heights of prosperity—and plunged it into deep depressions. Millions were migrating from farms and small towns to urban centers like New York and Chicago, where people found jobs in steel mills and department stores, and rubbed elbows with a stream of immigrants from Europe.

This was a new kind of world, which brought previously unimagined problems—and no ready solutions. But in some of those middle-class parlors, forward-thinking people—Ethel Percy Andrus among them—were taking note of the problems and resolving to do something about them.

simply an extension of what I daily was seeing in my father's life—a conviction that we must give of ourselves, to our fellows—must do some good, somewhere, for which we would receive no pay other than the satisfaction of the doing."

She attended Austin High School on Chicago's West Side from 1896 to 1900. "I enjoyed serving the school for two years as editor of the *Austin Voice* and one year as head of self-government," she would reflect in an autobiographical essay. She also played on the girls basketball team. Ethel left no details about her student government experience, but it must have been memorable: "I hate to admit that the next year self-government was abandoned!" the red-haired activist later wrote.

Relatively few Americans went to college in 1900, and few of those were women. The Andrus sisters were among the exceptions. Maud graduated in 1897 from the Chicago Normal School, a teachers college that was a hotbed of progressive education under its renowned principal, Francis W. Parker. Maud then taught in Chicago public schools, where she met fellow educator Emma M. Turner, who would be a lifelong friend of both Andrus sisters.

After graduating from Austin High School in 1900, Ethel enrolled at the University of Chicago, where she had won a scholarship. For an ambitious young woman with an urge to serve humanity, it would be the perfect destination.

ETHEL ARRIVED at the University of Chicago at the dawn of the Progressive Era. Its faculty featured John Dewey, a towering figure in American intellectual history. Dewey, a philosopher, cofounded the school of thought known as pragmatism. The idea: to examine the merit of ideas and policies based on their usefulness and practicality. He came to the university in 1894 as head of its philosophy department and founded an experimental school with his wife, Harriet, to test

INFLUENCES

PETER COOPER (TOP) OFFERED COLLEGE FREE FOR THE WORKING CLASS AND WOMEN. **JOHN DEWEY** PIONEERED HANDS-ON LEARNING.

his education theories. A charter member of the progressive education movement, Dewey believed that schools could help create a more democratic society by guiding the growth of children.

"Some few years ago I was looking about the school supply stores in the city, trying to find desks and chairs which seemed thoroughly suitable from all points of view—artistic, hygienic and educational—to the needs of the children," Dewey wrote in his 1899 book *The School and Society*. "We had a good deal of difficulty in finding what we needed, and finally one dealer, more intelligent than the rest, made this remark: 'I am afraid we have not what you want. You want something at which the children may work; these are all for listening.'"

For Dewey, the comment encapsulated the problem with traditional education: "The attitude of listening means, comparatively speaking, passivity, absorption," he found, using "ready-made materials ... prepared by the school superintendent, the board, the teacher, and of which the child is to take in as much as possible in the least possible time."

Rejecting this traditional, authoritarian approach to teaching, Dewey emphasized flexibility, spontaneity and democracy in the classroom. His experimental school in Chicago focused on learning through active engagement, rather than rote learning. Children learned biology, for example, by studying birds and animals, not just by memorizing their Latin names. Chemistry came to life by boiling maple syrup and watching it crystallize. Coal that heated the classrooms was traced back to fossil plants.

Ethel left no recollections about her interactions with Dewey, but he apparently made an impact. In September 1901, after a year at the university, she applied to a teacher training program—not at the U. of C. but at an affiliated school, the innovative Lewis Institute, on Chicago's near West Side.

Her College Years

THE LEWIS INSTITUTE is considered the first junior college in the United States. It was created in 1895 with a bequest from the late Chicago philanthropist Allen C. Lewis. The idea was to offer evening vocational classes for adults along with "a school for respectable females" who needed skills. William Rainey Harper, founding president of the University of Chicago, organized the new school. He chose George N. Carman, an English professor at the university, to serve as its first director. Carman recruited a colleague, Edwin H. Lewis, as the school's first dean of students. Both Carman and Lewis would become Ethel's lifelong mentors and friends.

Carman was Harper's protégé, a prominent educational reformer and an early champion of college accreditation. Edwin H. Lewis, Andrus' English teacher, helped shape the careers of noted journalists, among them Dorothy Thompson, dubbed by *Time* the second-most influential woman in America, after Eleanor Roosevelt.

Ethel credited Lewis with encouraging her to become a teacher, though she would make her mark in journalism, too, becoming the founding editor of the *NRTA Journal* and, later, *Modern Maturity*.

The Lewis Institute, a four-year high school and two-year college, was closely affiliated with the U. of C. in the early 1900s. Ethel attended them simultaneously while earning a four-year degree. She graduated in 1903 and immediately joined the institute faculty. She taught English and German for seven happy, busy years.

Ethel at the Lewis Institute

MENTORS

GEORGE N. CARMAN (TOP) PIONEERED JUNIOR COLLEGES. **EDWIN H. LEWIS,** AN INSPIRATIONAL ENGLISH PROFESSOR, URGED ETHEL TO TEACH.

CHICAGO WAS A TURBULENT town at the start of the 20th century. The Progressive Era was in full flower, as genteel reformers battled corrupt machine politicians and arrogant robber barons for the city's soul. This was the Chicago of *The Jungle,* Upton Sinclair's 1906 novel about miserable conditions facing immigrants and others who worked in the city's meatpacking industry, fed by its sprawling stockyards. Yet Chicago was also dynamic, alive with energy and bursting with new residents as it challenged New York for national urban supremacy.

By this point, Ethel was living with her family in the suburb of Oak Park, a short streetcar ride west from the Lewis Institute. Even here she found thriving cultural action. Oak Park boasted many buildings designed by Frank Lloyd Wright, whose home and studio, the cradle of modern architecture, stood less than a mile from her parents' house. And close by lay the boyhood home of the novelist Ernest Hemingway—born in Oak Park in 1899 and educated in local schools. Ray Kroc, the future McDonald's founder, was also born there, in 1902.

As a young teacher, Ethel was particularly enthusiastic about a drama group she directed at the Lewis Institute. With her commitment to giving back, Ethel had her actors occasionally perform for audiences who could not afford theater tickets and may not have understood English.

"We want to remind you that our play will be given Saturday evening, April second, at a quarter past eight, at the Commons," she wrote in a note to George Carman in March 1904. The significance lies in the venue: the Chicago Commons, a settlement house within walking distance of the Lewis Institute. The audience would consist mostly of poor immigrants still struggling to find their footing in America. To help guide these people toward better lives, Chicago progressives were creating settlement houses like the Commons and Jane Addams' Hull House, another place where Ethel's troupes performed. At Hull House, Ethel finally crossed paths with the indomitable Addams.

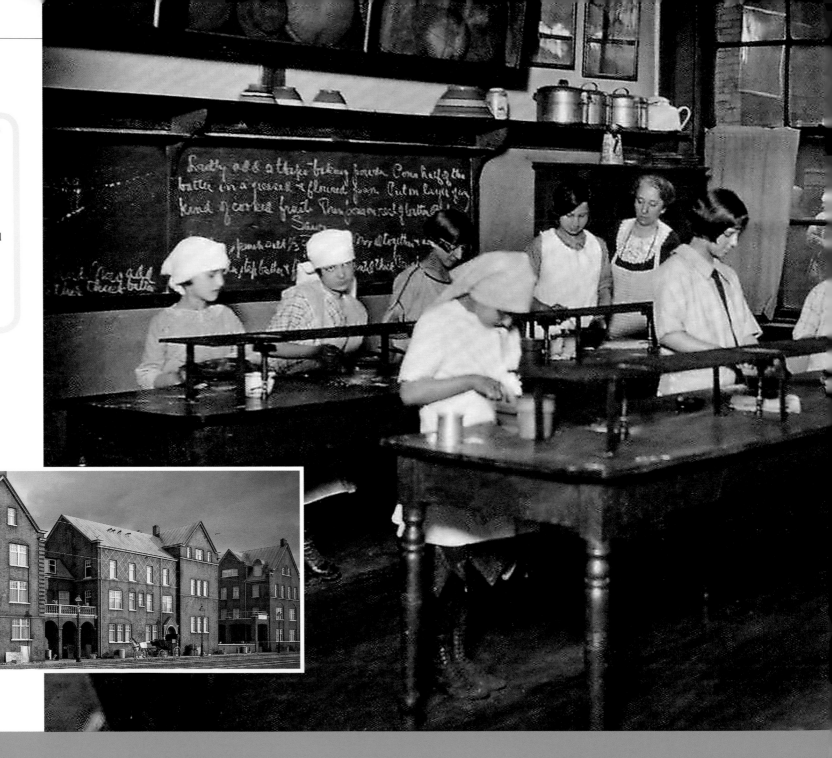

Hull House

Hull House, where Ethel volunteered in the afternoons, after teaching at the Lewis institute

JANE ADDAMS was an Illinois heiress with a highly developed social conscience who wanted to make a difference in the world. In 1889 she and her friend Ellen Gates Starr founded Hull House, which served immigrants in an impoverished Chicago neighborhood.

The settlement houses were experiments in communal living. They recruited highly educated, well-to-do reformers to move in and teach useful skills to local immigrants. Jane Addams' friend John Dewey sat on the board (and later modeled his experimental lab school on the Hull House kindergarten). She also offered night-school classes for adults, focusing on subjects such as English, citizenship and the arts.

After teaching classes at the Lewis Institute, Ethel spent her afternoons as a part-time volunteer at Hull House and the Commons. "I learned there to know life intimately and to value folks of different races and creeds," she would recall. In the 1890s, Hull House was located in the midst of a densely populated urban neighborhood peopled by Italian, Irish, German, Greek, Bohemian, and Russian and Polish Jewish immigrants. "I learned to respect their pride, and to enjoy their humor, to know their innate dignity, to marvel at their resourcefulness in adversity and their great and supporting faith. I saw their wonderful examples—not only of rehabilitation but of resurrection, as well. Together, my teaching and my volunteer work made for me a very happy and wonderful life."

Ethel also made an important connection with another volunteer, Kate Crane Gartz, whose father, industrialist and philanthropist Richard T. Crane, was a major financial backer of Hull House. This Gartz connection would later loom large in Ethel's life.

> "We were very insistent that the Settlement should not be primarily for children and that it was absurd to suppose that grown people would not respond to opportunities for education and social life."
>
> *–Jane Addams, founder of Hull House*

Return to California

ETHEL TREMENDOUSLY enjoyed her life in Chicago. She might have spent her entire career there, but in 1909 she and her father became ill. (Records don't specify the type of illness, although in one letter she said she felt weak.) That winter, she took a sabbatical from the Lewis Institute to accompany her family on a trip to Southern California.

"I know in due gratefulness for my leave I should say that I am feeling better already, but the truth is that every day I feel more tired," Ethel wrote in a letter to George Carman early in 1910 from Santa Paula, a small town northwest of Los Angeles. "But this cannot keep on forever in this land of winter sunshine and roses."

Her own health eventually improved, but her father grew worse.

"A gracious physician gave me my first close-up view when he said to me, 'Your father is suffering from atrophy of the optic nerve. Just how soon he will be blind, I can't say, but I suggest that you plan for his care and happiness with the knowledge that the disease is a progressive one.' It was then I realized the possible bleakness of enforced and unexpected retirement."

For the sake of George Andrus' health, the family stayed in Santa Paula, where his daughters became the family breadwinners. Maud found a job at the local library while Ethel began teaching at Santa Paula High School. Both Andrus sisters were still single and verging on spinsterhood by early-20th-century standards. When the 1910 census enumerator came to the door, they shaved several years off their ages—which seems ironic given Ethel's future role as an antiageism crusader. Maud eventually started using her actual birth year of 1878, but for the rest of her life, Ethel gave hers as 1884. (Her birth certificate may have been lost in the fire that followed the 1906 San Francisco earthquake, but recent research indicates she was born in 1881.)

Whatever her age, Ethel clearly was old enough to live on her own. She could have returned to Chicago and the Lewis Institute, where Carman had planned to promote her to assistant registrar. But she was close to her family. Her father needed her. Reluctantly, she decided to resign.

"I hated to write you this letter that would sever my connection with my two greatest benefactors, you and Dr. Lewis, and the institution I hold the dearest on earth," she wrote Carman. Another mentor, Edwin Lewis, reassured Ethel that she should remain in California with her family. "We need have no regrets, no backward glances" when doing what is right, he wrote her in May 1910.

Santa Paula was hardly San Francisco. Ethel's once-brilliant career prospects seemed blighted. Chicago was the epicenter of the progressive education movement; Santa Paula was an isolated town in the Ventura County backcountry.

She didn't stay in Santa Paula long. In November 1910 she applied for a job at Manual Arts High School, a brand-new school in Los Angeles, where a brand-new metropolis was taking shape.

RESIGNATION EDWIN LEWIS OFFERED ETHEL COMFORT AND UNDERSTANDING.

Ethel (circled) with the staff of Manual Arts High School in Los Angeles

CHAPTER 2

"OPPORTUNITY PRO

Andrus' drama students—including Robert Young as Robin Hood—performing at Lincoln High School

Lincoln High School, where Andrus served as principal for nearly 28 years

Lincoln High: Transforming a community

MISED"

FEW AMERICANS ATTENDED school past eighth grade in the 1800s, and many who did went to private academies serving the college-bound elite. Now, with more teenagers going to high school, fast-growing cities such as Los Angeles were building new schools and adjusting the curricula to serve students from working-class families. Manual Arts High, which opened in 1910, offered classes in drafting, metalworking and basic mechanics, but many teachers at traditional high schools were reluctant to work there. Not so for Ethel Percy Andrus.

She started teaching English at Manual Arts High in 1911, and she taught it well, as many former students would attest in later years. Some became her lifelong friends, and at least two would make their marks on the world: Goodwin Knight and General James Doolittle. Knight became a judge, went into politics and served as California governor, from 1953 to 1959. Doolittle became an aviation pioneer and in World War II led the famous Doolittle Raid, in which his squadron of B-25 bombers took off from an aircraft carrier and attacked targets in Japan, avenging the surprise attack on Pearl Harbor.

Andrus' reputation in the classroom traveled all the way back to Chicago, where the 1916 Lewis Institute yearbook described her as "the most popular teacher in California." She also acquired administration experience at Manual Arts by filling in for a semester as vice principal for girls. Evidently she performed with distinction, for when the same position became open at another new Los Angeles school, the district offered her the job. She joined the administration at Abraham Lincoln High in February 1916, in the middle of the school year. By the following September, she was promoted to principal.

Andrus' "Opportunity" gate welcomed students of all ages.

Lincoln High Years

INCOLN HIGH was founded in 1913, in a neighborhood then known as East Los Angeles. More than 1,000 students attended Lincoln in 1916, when Andrus became the first woman to run a major urban high school in California. (The state's previous woman principals mostly had managed rural or small-town schools with fewer students.) At Lincoln High, Andrus faced the daunting challenge of serving an increasingly diverse, multilingual population—students and their families spoke more than a dozen languages. These working-class immigrants from Russia, Asia and Latin America poured into East Los Angeles, replacing the middle-class Anglo families migrating westward to Hollywood and beyond.

Lincoln had been built high atop a hill, isolating it from the community. To overcome that isolation, Andrus held "Community Nights" twice a month, with guest speakers and sing-alongs to draw in locals. She wanted residents to view Lincoln High as the hub of their community. Evidence of her quick success came in March 1917, only six months into her tenure as principal, when 1,000 citizens at a Community Night voted unanimously to change the neighborhood's name to Lincoln Heights. When Los Angeles officials approved the change, Andrus officiated at the ceremony that marked the community's rechristening.

At Lincoln, Andrus drew upon lessons she had learned from her Chicago mentors to transform the school into something akin to Hull House. She wanted the school to

Power Machine — Miss Cordner

Furniture Upholstery — Mr. MacKenzie

Dressmaking — Mrs. Gruwell

emphasize learning rather than teaching—to shift the focus from what teachers did to what students did. She developed innovative programs that guided students to be their own teachers and to learn by doing.

One of the first things that Andrus did as principal was to spell the word "opportunity" in big letters over the school's entrance gate. She meant opportunity for everyone, not just students going on to college but also those—the majority—whose formal education would end when they graduated from Lincoln. Some traditional academic subjects, like Latin and Greek, were of little use to students who aspired to be nurses or auto mechanics. Andrus made the curriculum more relevant to the future needs of her students, and she enthusiastically embraced the idea of vocational education.

Andrus' arrival at Lincoln was well timed: In February 1917, Congress passed the Smith-Hughes Vocational Education Act, which provided funds for schools to hire local artisans to teach students their crafts. "Latin and Greek gave way to Smith-Hughes courses in trades and industries," Andrus later said. "Indeed, when the history of vocational education in the Southwest is written, Lincoln will write the first chapter. A truly cosmopolitan school, it grew into a school of opportunity for college members and the artisans."

Andrus made sure the curriculum served all students, not just those who aspired to become doctors or lawyers or engineers. She also made sure that students from non-academic backgrounds could aspire to become a doctor or a lawyer or an engineer, if they so chose. Andrus did not want to push students toward predetermined destinations; she wanted to give them the mental tools to plot their own course in life.

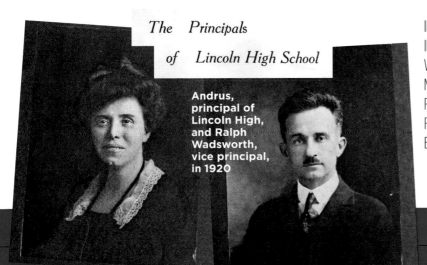

The Principals of Lincoln High School

Andrus, principal of Lincoln High, and Ralph Wadsworth, vice principal, in 1920

INNOVATIONS IN EDUCATION

VOCATIONAL CLASSES, NEW AT THE TIME, PREPARED MALE AND FEMALE STUDENTS TO EARN A LIVING.

Spurring Social Change

ATHLETICS

DRAMA

MUSIC

ANDRUS' SCHOOL served a changing neighborhood increasingly dominated by immigrants from Italy, Russia, China and Mexico. She made it her mission to help students from other lands become full-fledged Americans without turning their backs on their family heritage.

"Our faith became an obsession," she recalled. "We must keep our many nationalities conscious and proud of their racial and national background, of the contributions those made to the American dream and, likewise, to the insistent obligation they, the youngsters, must themselves accept in raising their own coming families with a double loyalty—respecting their own roots and the traditions alike of America, and the land and faith of their forefathers."

The first step was to encourage school spirit.

"The situation was a grave one," Andrus remembered. "We were without school spirit, and school spirit is to a school what patriotism is to one's country. ... With this spirit the school is vibrant, constructive; without it, a mere aggregation of boys and girls. But our problem was how to get this school spirit that would hold, unify, uplift and sustain us, that would be our unifying religion."

The answer came naturally to Andrus, a former varsi-

EXTRACURRICULARS AT LINCOLN INSTILLED SCHOOL SPIRIT. ⟶

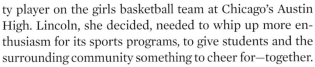

Ethel Says

"[Students] read books on etiquette, carefully minded their manners— and so did I. I don't now, but I did then."

ty player on the girls basketball team at Chicago's Austin High. Lincoln, she decided, needed to whip up more enthusiasm for its sports programs, to give students and the surrounding community something to cheer for—together.

At first, Lincoln's teams still did poorly. But with Andrus leading the cheers, the students rallied behind the athletes and began to feel part of a larger team comprising the entire student body.

She created an inspirational litany for the students to recite at the beginning of each Lincoln assembly in the auditorium. It echoed the Declaration of Independence and reflected Andrus' egalitarian, multicultural viewpoint: "I hold these truths to be self-evident: that all men are created equal. God hath made of one blood all races of men, and we are his children, brothers and sisters all."

WHEN ANDRUS arrived at Lincoln High, the school was plagued by high rates of truancy and delinquency. High-spirited teenagers who were not academically inclined found mandatory schooling a challenge, and the problem was exacerbated at Lincoln, where so many students were working-class immigrants from places where formal schooling was not a tradition. Making the curriculum more useful to them helped Andrus reduce those rates, as did her use of sports to boost school spirit and her effective use of guidance counselors to help students make good choices. (She received help from her sister, Maud, who joined the Lincoln staff as a teacher in the mid-1920s and retired from the school 20 years later as head counselor.)

But Ethel Andrus did not stop there. She offered plenty of social activities at Lincoln, and she structured them in ways that turned potential troublemakers into useful citizens through social learning. To an unusual degree for a high school of that time, Lincoln offered a wide range of school activities: clubs, school plays and concerts, dances and pageants. Andrus also created the "Low and Lonesome" club, in which socially active students befriended those who felt isolated or lacked confidence; and the student-run Junior Coordinating Council, which sent students into the community as volunteers.

"Our student body became part of the larger social movements of Lincoln Heights," Andrus wrote. "Recognition for civic performance satisfied and fed the drives of youth, which like age wants to be needed, to be praised, and to 'be a member of the team.'"

Andrus' programs were praised as models for reducing truancy and delinquency rates. But it was not just the programs Andrus devised that kept students in school; it was also the effect she had on them.

"Somehow you found yourself acting the way she wanted you to," one former troublemaker recalled.

The new faces of Los Angeles, from the 1926 Lincoln High School yearbook

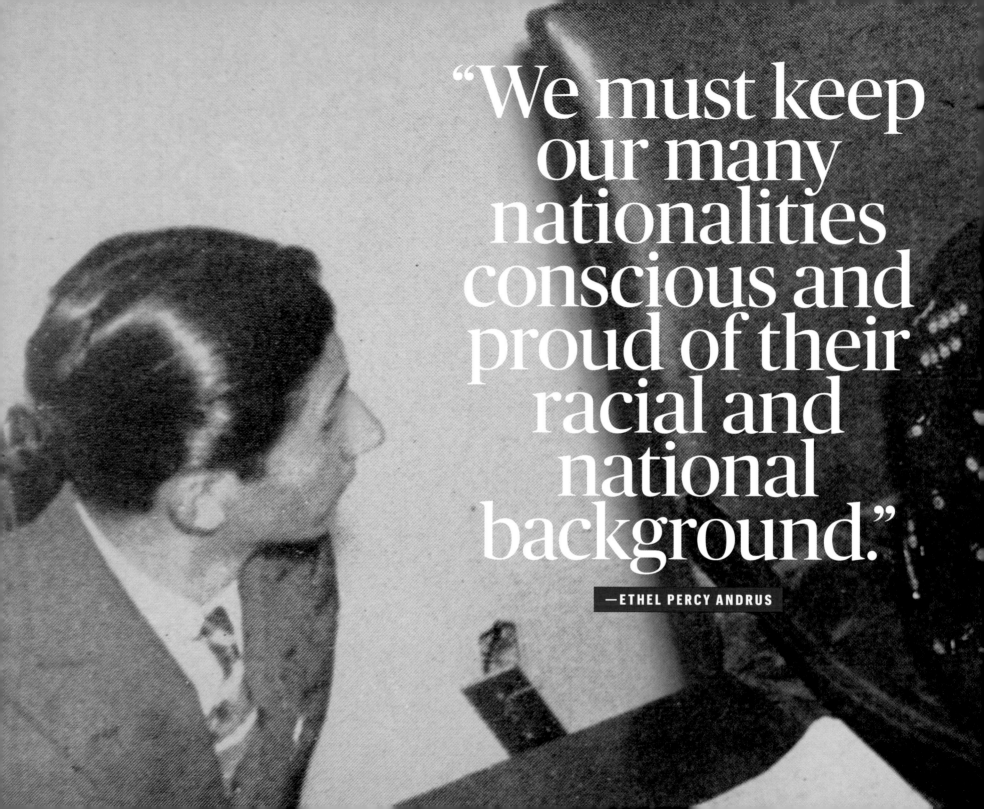

"We must keep our many nationalities conscious and proud of their racial and national background."

—ETHEL PERCY ANDRUS

WHEN ANDRUS placed the word "opportunity" atop the school's entrance gate, she wanted to inspire not only students but also their parents. She set out to create an Opportunity School that would offer evening classes to local adults. This was her chance to emulate her childhood hero Peter Cooper by creating her own version of his Cooper Union. Full of enthusiasm, she pitched her idea to the Los Angeles Board of Education.

"Here we met a snag," she recalled.

The Board of Education rejected her idea, claiming it wasn't worth the cost because not enough adults in that neighborhood would be willing to climb that steep hill at night to take classes.

"I believed otherwise," Andrus remembered. "I sold the board the idea that if they would allow me the light and heat, I would assume the responsibility for no increase in janitors' cost [and] I would also provide a faculty and administration and a student body."

The board relented, and Andrus delivered on her promise. Her Opportunity School opened with a faculty drawn mostly from the ranks of neighborhood artisans and professionals, plus Andrus herself and one other Lincoln High teacher. She induced a French Baptist minister to teach French, a department store's Spanish interpreter to teach Spanish and the Los Angeles Fire Department's superintendent of car barns to teach machine-shop skills. She controlled costs yet created a program that enticed many grown-up students to trudge up all those stairs to attend the classes and earn the equivalency of a high school diploma. The Opportunity School was a major success and eventually evolved into the Lincoln Heights Adult Evening School. It paid an unexpected dividend when many of the night-school teachers Andrus had recruited from the community "with official status and salary became teachers by day, as well," she recollected.

ANOTHER SUCCESSFUL Andrus innovation was *The World Hour,* a weekly hour-long program presented to Lincoln students during assembly. Andrus assigned its preparation to drama teacher Edward Wenig (who later would work for Andrus at the National Retired Teachers Association and the American Association of Retired Persons).

"*The World Hour* employed the technique of the living newspaper, acquainting students with important developments throughout the world," Wenig said. "The format was usually that of a radio broadcast, with students acting as announcers and performing dramatizations of important events involving current newsmakers."

Wenig and his drama students also produced a companion program, *The Lincoln Hour,* which highlighted the contributions different ethnic groups made to American culture. "It attempted to relieve the tensions and conflicts that arose among students of foreign parentage as they tried to find their places in the American scene," Wenig said.

One of Wenig's drama club stars was the future stage and screen luminary Robert Preston. Andrus made a deep impression on him.

"Even before I enrolled in Lincoln High, I used to pass the gate at the entrance of the school on the hill and wonder about the word OPPORTUNITY in huge letters on the arch," Preston would recall. "By graduation time we all knew the full meaning of the word. What better word could Dr. Andrus have used to greet

"**School spirit is to a school what patriotism is to one's country.**"

–*Ethel Percy Andrus*

The 1933 earthquake damaged buildings in the school complex. Below right: Andrus' yearbook message addressed that year's seniors, who would be the last group to graduate from the original campus before it was demolished.

the entering students of all races and creeds? Then, too, how thrilling it must have been for the parents living in the Lincoln Heights district to know that their boys and girls were privileged to learn of the opportunity promised them as they climbed up the 102 steps to the auditorium and to learn from their principal the full meaning of the promise!"

When Lincoln's original hilltop campus was severely damaged by the 1933 Long Beach earthquake, the school board wanted to rebuild it in another location. Andrus, her students and the local community fought to keep the school where it was, and they won—the new school was built right next to the old one.

To the Seniors

DR. ETHEL PERCY ANDRUS, *Principal*

... Your passing marks the close of an era in the history of your school. A new site, new buildings, new faces may tend to make the new Lincoln a strange place, beautiful, efficient, serviceable but not home, not intimately yours as are these buildings and grounds. I beg of you, however, to search and find in the new buildings and the new site the Lincoln of your memory and dreams. The bulletin board in your main hall challenges you. Do you remember its wording?

"I am more than wood and brick and stone, more than flesh and blood – I am the composite soul of all who call me home; I am your school." So I beg of you to think of her faring on – as dear in your love there in her new site as here on the hill. Think of her as the same, and say she is still my school. She is Alma Mater."

Notable Students

KENNY WASHINGTON *(1918-1971)* was a Lincoln High football hero who starred at UCLA in the same backfield with Jackie Robinson. When Washington signed a contract with the Los Angeles Rams in 1946, he, with teammate Woody Strode, ended the National Football League's 13-year ban that had kept African Americans from playing in the league. A year later, Robinson integrated Major League Baseball.

SADAO MUNEMORI
(*1922-1945*) served in World War II while his family was in the Manzanar internment camp for Japanese Americans. He earned a posthumous Medal of Honor for throwing himself onto a German grenade to save two comrades.

JOSÉ LIMÓN
(*1908-1972*) immigrated to Los Angeles from Mexico as a child and later starred on Broadway as a dancer. Both as a performer and as a choreographer, he is considered a crucial figure in modern dance.

ROBERT PRESTON
(*1918-1987*) credited Andrus for insisting that the drama students tackle Shakespeare, rather than settling for less demanding plays. He enjoyed a long career in Hollywood and on Broadway. He is best remembered as Professor Harold Hill in *The Music Man*.

ROBERT YOUNG
(*1907-1998*) went on to a long career as a leading man in Hollywood. He is best known for starring in two long-running television shows: *Father Knows Best* and *Marcus Welby, M.D.*

Caregiving Beckons

"Education is a social process; education is growth; education is not a preparation for life but is life itself."

—*John Dewey*

Family photo, from left: Maud, Ethel and their mother, Lucretia

ETHEL PERCY ANDRUS had absorbed that philosophy while studying for her bachelor's degree at the University of Chicago, and she preached it for decades to teachers and students at Lincoln High School. She also followed her own advice. Andrus was a lifelong learner, in both the formal and informal senses of the word.

In 1928 she earned a master's degree from the University of Southern California, after writing her thesis on leadership training. Two years later, the USC School of Education awarded her a Ph.D. Dr. Andrus, as she would henceforth be known, titled her dissertation "The Development of an Educational Program for the High-School Girl Based on a Critical Study of Her Nature and Her Needs." She had essentially been researching this subject for 27 years, since she started teaching at the Lewis Institute back in 1903.

"The modern age with its industrial revolution and the World War has freed women from economic parasitism," she wrote in her dissertation. "The 20th century has seen in the span of one lifetime, women, be they spinsters, wives or mothers, attain recognition as differentiated individuals, worthy of respect as entities, with the right and a sense of responsibility to selves and the laws of their own evolutionary, spiritual growth."

Her dissertation, while focusing on high school girls' education, also exhibited Dr. Andrus' commitment to equal rights for all in body, mind and spirit. She referred to the need for "progress toward the still tardy goal of man's recognition of woman as a ... complementary human being ... entitled to develop her own individuality and to follow her own ends."

Dr. Andrus never stopped learning and never stopped teaching, even after she moved up to the principal's office. During summer breaks from her duties at Lincoln, she taught courses at UCLA, the University of Southern California and Stanford University. Nor was her influence limited to the classroom. Through her lectures, her articles in education journals and her membership on the National Education Association's Educational Policies Commission, Dr. Andrus continued to advocate for progressive education, holding up Lincoln High as a model for other schools to emulate.

BY THE SPRING OF 1944, Dr. Andrus had been Lincoln's principal for almost 28 years. At age 62 she showed no signs of slowing down or wanting to move on to new challenges. She was thoroughly devoted to her students. And yet, on a Tuesday morning in June during the last week of the semester, she arrived at a scheduled school staff meeting and abruptly announced her retirement.

"My resignation came to Lincoln and to myself as a sudden surprise," she would later write.

Her father had died in 1920, and her mother's health had been declining for several years.

"That morning, the nurse attending my mother told me her belief that my mother was to be a hopeless invalid," Dr. Andrus recollected. "On the way to school, I determined that I could give to her the loving care she had given to my father during his blindness. I knew I could bring her back, so that day I resigned."

"You can't do this to us," her school district superior protested.

"My mother needs me now," she replied. And that was that. As she had back in Santa Paula in 1910, she put her family above her career and left a school she loved to take up her new role as her mother's caregiver. She did not know it, but her sudden decision would launch her on an unexpected new career, one that transformed how Americans think about retirement.

"The fact that [my mother] recovered, and later urged my doing for older folks what I had with great good fortune been able to do for her, is proof that I was right," Dr. Andrus wrote. "I have never regretted it."

> # "My resignation came to Lincoln and to myself as a sudden surprise."
>
> –Ethel Percy Andrus

RETIREMENT PLANS

When she retired in 1944, Ethel Percy Andrus had earned a modest monthly retirement benefit of $85.42 per month (a $61.49 pension and a $23.93 annuity). Neither was adjusted for inflation. Her pension was a little higher than a teacher's pension, which was, on average, $40.

RETIREMENT SYSTEM
LOS ANGELES CITY SCHOOLS

NOTICE OF RETIREMENT ON REGULAR ALLOWANCE

September 22_____, 1944

Dr. Ethel Percy Andrus

314 Kenneth Road

Glendale 2, California

Dear Dr. Andrus:

Your application for retirement effective_____August 1, 1944_____is approved. Your retirement allowance will be $85.42_____per calendar month payable to you for life. Payment for the months of August and September will be made on the first day of October_____, 19 44 , and thereafter on the first day of each month.

Very truly yours,

RETIREMENT BOARD OF THE
LOS ANGELES CITY SCHOOL DISTRICT

By_____
ASSISTANT SUPERINTENDENT

INCOME TAX INFORMATION

Cost of Member's Annuity $2,822.94
Retirement Allowance:
   District's Pension $ 61.49
   Member's Annuity $ 23.93
   Total Monthly Retirement Allowance $ 85.42
It is IMPORTANT that this information be retained for Federal and State Income Tax purposes. No future statements will be sent. For assistance in preparing your Federal Income Tax, consult The Bureau of Internal Revenue.

CHAPTER 3

"TO LIVE IN DI

NRTA's early
offices were in
Ojai, California.
Dr. Andrus
allowed staff to
work flexible
schedules.

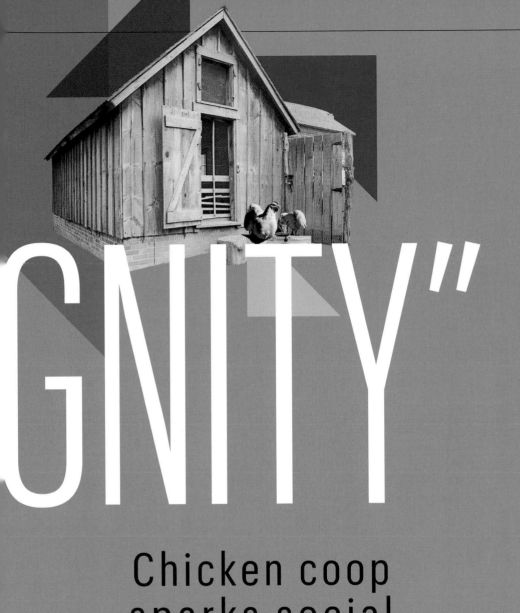

GNITY"

Chicken coop sparks social movement

EVEN BEFORE her retirement from Lincoln High School, Dr. Ethel Percy Andrus had stumbled across the path to her next career, although she couldn't have realized where it would lead. She had just accepted an assignment from the Association of California Secondary School Principals, a group she had cofounded. In the past she had served as president; now she was offered a job that seemed like a step down.

"They gave their only woman member the most inane assignment—that of welfare," she later recalled.

California had established a retirement plan for teachers, paying, on average, $40 a month. Even with that sum, teachers struggled. And for many, that was their sole income; female teachers were often single because, until 1927, California school boards could fire them for getting married. That meager pension, Dr. Andrus wrote, left retired schoolteachers "without adequate funds to keep alive, much less to live in dignity." Her new job: "to ferret out these unfortunates and to see that they did not become objects of public charity."

A worthy assignment, but it had nothing to do with education policy, Dr. Andrus' area of expertise. As former president of the Association of California Secondary School Principals, she had, along with her male peers, played a leadership role in developing education policy.

"I knew [the new task] only as a humanitarian operation and wondered just what might be my contribution to it," she said. "I had not long to wait."

One Saturday, she received a telephone call from a shopkeeper in the nearby town of La Habra. A former teacher was in poor health, the shopkeeper said. Dr. Andrus drove to the address and found nobody home.

The man next door told Dr. Andrus the resident of the pleasant bungalow she had approached was not elderly and not in need. "Then, just as he was dismissing me," Dr. Andrus related, "he recalled that there was an old woman who lived next door, 'in back,' in the chicken house. ...

"I knocked on the sagging door of the windowless shed and assured the answering voice that I had come to say 'Howdy'—one teacher to another. ... I waited for the door to open and when it did, my hostess slipped through and closed the door behind her. ...

"'Just a friendly visit,' I said, and I told her my name. Curiously enough, she knew it, and more curiously, I recognized hers when she told me it, and recalled her reputation as a Spanish teacher of some distinction.

"When I asked if we might chat under cover out of the drizzle, she waved me to my car, and there she told me her story. Thriftily she had saved money enough to buy, on installments, some scenic acreage in Montrose, a charming section above Glendale. ... But, alas, the Depression took away all opportunity for sale, and a devastating flood washed away the approaches to the property.

"She saw her high hopes disappear with it. ... She still had her $40 a month to live on, and courageously she decided to make that do. She dropped from her friends' sight and memory."

That visit would have a profound impact on Dr. Andrus and her life's work. When Dr. Andrus' mother recovered, she urged her daughter to devote herself to the elderly, as she formerly had devoted herself to high school students.

"Old age, Ethel, needs care as youth needs care, but it needs something more," Lucretia Andrus told her daughter. "It needs the desire to live, to continue planning and striving hopefully, to keep working at something worthwhile, and then when, at last, old age becomes dependent, it needs someone to still care, or if there is no one to care, there should be community care, which can make it easy to help those who now cannot help themselves to keep their dignity and their self-respect."

Inspired, Dr. Andrus embarked on a second career, as an advocate for retired educators.

Founding of NRTA

ANDRUS LAUNCHED her new career in her mid-60s, an age when workers often faced mandatory retirement. Many teachers were unsettled by the forced transition. They had entered the profession during the heady days of the Progressive Era. They had set out to make the world a better place. Now they felt that the world had discarded them.

"Teachers' salaries had been low, but the challenge of the teacher's calling had given us dignity and social stature and prestige," Dr. Andrus wrote. "Now, our occupation gone, we felt no longer wanted, needed or regarded; the retired teachers were heartsick, often lacking purpose, self-confidence and faith."

As welfare director of the California Teachers Association, Southern Section, Dr. Andrus helped raise money to expand the Southern California Teachers Home in Pasadena, which provided subsidized group housing for low-income retired teachers. As a member of the California Retired Teachers Association, she lobbied the state legislature for higher pensions. In the course of all this, she began to envision what retired teachers could accomplish if they formed a national organization.

As she had done in her years at Lincoln High, Dr. Andrus recognized a need and found a solution. Employing her enthusiasm and powers of persuasion, she decided to found the National Retired Teachers Association to give retired teachers a national forum to advocate for pension reform, tax benefits, housing improvements and health insurance coverage, and to continue their support of education. Before NRTA, most advocacy efforts for retired teachers occurred at the state level. NRTA was designed to work closely with the state retired teachers associations, giving them a nationwide voice.

Dr. Andrus had to employ her formidable powers of leadership and persuasion to convince the independent state organizations that they should join forces and work cooperatively on a national agenda. But she persisted and, on October 13, 1947, NRTA was founded in Berkeley, California, at a meeting of the California Retired Teachers Association. Dr. Andrus was elected president.

During the early years, she and her friend and fellow educator Ruth Lana ran NRTA from the house they shared in Glendale with Dr. Andrus' mother and Lana's daughter, Lora.

"We had a large kitchen in the back," Lora remembered many years later. "That's where it all started, that's where all the work was done." To be more precise, NRTA's cradle was the little breakfast room next to the kitchen.

"It was very small, but we didn't have very many people," Ruth Lana said. "So that's where we kept the files and did the work."

Dr. Andrus set individual membership dues at $1. Her reasoning stemmed from an incident that occurred following a speech she gave to raise support for the creation of NRTA. Upon hearing of the plight of the nation's re-

"NRTA is built upon the thesis that creative energy is ageless."

–*Ethel Percy Andrus*

National Retired Teachers Association
Dupont Circle Building ● Washington 6, D. C.

Honoring Founding Member
EVIDENCE OF MEMBERSHIP

Dr. Ethel Percy Andrus
600 E. Ocean Blvd., #905
Long Beach, California

SIGNATURE OF MEMBER

NATIONAL RETIRED TEACHERS ASSOCIATION
1947
FOUNDED 1947
INCORPORATED
JUNE 18, 1952
Ethel Percy Andrus
PRESIDENT

DR. ANDRUS' NRTA MEMBERSHIP CARD ⟶

tired teachers, an acquaintance handed Dr. Andrus a dollar bill and said, "Here are my dues." That was a good indication, she decided, of what other teachers could probably afford.

SHE ESTABLISHED FOUR PURPOSES FOR NRTA

1 To promote the professional, social and economic status of retired teachers
2 To afford opportunity for the investigation of and interchange of opinions on subjects of special interest to retired teachers
3 To further the advancement of education in the United States
4 To seek a dynamic relationship with the National Education Association and to support its programs

By 1950, NRTA was firmly established with 500 members. The first national convention was held that year in St. Louis. In August they won their first legislative battle when Congress excluded members of existing state or local pension plans from Social Security, since school district employees (among other state, county and municipal workers) were already covered by their own retirement systems. Switching teachers from their pre-existing pension systems to Social Security would have resulted in smaller monthly checks. Dr. Andrus and her colleagues were instrumental in this victory through articles and editorials in the *NRTA Quarterly* and speeches across the country.

By 1952, NRTA and other organizations were working on a campaign to exempt retirement income from federal taxes. When Dr. Andrus testified before the House Ways and Means Committee in 1953, she explained that retired teachers were paying income taxes on annuities that were being eaten up by inflation. Between June 1940 and June 1952, she said, the average teacher's annuity increased "a little over 35 percent, but the price index for that same period had advanced nearly 89 percent."

Paying annual income taxes left some retired teachers without enough money for living expenses, she said:

Early Advocacy Victories

AUGUST 1950
First legislative victory protects teachers from replacing higher state and local pensions with lower federal Social Security benefits.

AUGUST 1953
Dr. Andrus testifies in Congress that retired teachers have trouble paying federal taxes because inflation is eating up their pensions.

JULY 1950
NRTA's first annual convention is held in St. Louis. Membership: 500

JULY 1951
NRTA Legislative Council is created to advocate for retired teachers' interests.

1951–54
NRTA Legislative Council members visit Congress 20 times to press for tax relief for retired teachers.

"Some are viewing with hopeless dismay the gulf narrowing between the dignity of self-respecting support and the shock of acknowledged indigence."

The following year, Congress passed a bill supported by NRTA that shielded up to $1,200 of retirement pay from federal income tax for teachers and other retirees not covered by the Social Security system. "The legislative victory of a tax-exemption credit of $1,200—although not the full goal sought—heightened the tempo of our professional enthusiasm and activity," Dr. Andrus wrote.

She and her NRTA colleagues were proving that retired teachers, working together, could protect their financial security and enjoy a renewed sense that their lives had meaning and purpose. "The NRTA," Dr. Andrus would recall, "was and is built upon the thesis that creative energy is ageless—that we must keep on being active—that our years of experience, understanding and skill are reserves of energy and power that we must put to work to build richer, more interesting lives, to help stretch the purchasing power of the retirement dollars, to help in crusades that reach beyond the here and now and to find in such activity content, faith and hope."

Ethel Says

"I like the word 'old.' We feel it's a victory, not a defeat."

NOVEMBER 1954
NRTA's regional conference is held in the music room of Grey Gables in Ojai, California.

AUGUST 1954
Congress grants a tax-exemption credit of up to $1,200 to retired people, including teachers.

KEY ALLIES

RUTH LANA

Ruth Lana was a close friend and associate of Dr. Andrus. They met in California when Lana was a math teacher and Dr. Andrus headed Lincoln High. Lana and her daughter, Lora, lived with Dr. Andrus and her mother for years after Lana's divorce.

"I'm a follow-the-leader type of person, and Dr. Andrus was a leader," Lana recalled. "She realized the concerns for the people who are going to enter the next century. And she did something about it."

Lana's many contributions included heading NRTA's drug buying service and travel service and, later, serving as honorary president of the American Association of Retired Persons.

DOROTHY CRIPPEN

Dorothy Crippen was a first cousin of Ethel Percy Andrus. She taught school in her hometown of Palo Alto, California, for 36 years. After retiring, she helped build NRTA and headed Grey Gables (its retired teachers home) and the Acacias (a convalescent facility).

In the 1960s she took on increasingly senior roles in the management of key NRTA-AARP charitable, business and historical initiatives.

"She was dignified, poised, educated, competent, kind and a fighter," said Ruth Lana's son-in-law, Monty Warren, at her funeral, in 1982.

GRACE HATFIELD

A career educator in Missouri and Florida, Grace Hatfield was tapped by Dr. Andrus to manage NRTA's group health plan. Dr. Andrus noted her no-nonsense style: "Inspiring as she was in her classroom, and efficient as an office assistant, we of NRTA know her as a friend. ... We honor her for her eloquent example of activity after retirement." Hatfield would be with Dr. Andrus (and Ernest Giddings, associate legislative director of the National Education Association) in 1958 when she decided to create a new organization, the American Association of Retired Persons.

A New Retirement Community Experience

BUSY AS SHE was with NRTA, Dr. Andrus still served as welfare director for the California Teachers Association. In that role, she had led the push to expand the teachers retirement home in Pasadena, adding room for another 88 units, thanks to a 1950 bequest. Here was a solution to the problem of social isolation that plagued so many retired teachers. A large number were women who lived alone, either because they were widows or because they had never married. With no workplace to go to each day, they often were lonely, like the woman in the chicken coop who had lost contact with her former friends and colleagues.

"The fact that in the Southern California Teachers Home there were happily adjusted older folk who were alive and growing, mellow and sweet ... induced me to feel that what Southern California was doing for its oldsters, someone should be planning for those not living in the Southern California area," Dr. Andrus recalled.

Fun and fitness: Grey Gables had a heated pool.

That someone, unsurprisingly, would be Ethel Percy Andrus. In 1952 she proposed that NRTA establish a national teachers retirement home. To help teachers envision vibrant living, she published several articles about innovative housing options in the *NRTA Quarterly*. One of the articles outlined safety features, such as entry ramps and safe bathrooms, motor villages and cooperative apartments. Another was titled "Homes for Retired Teachers at Our Great Universities."

At year's end, Dr. Andrus explained why housing was so important.

"More than anything in this world it seems the average oldster wants to have a fitting place in which to live—tailored to his needs and planned within his budget," she wrote. "He is concerned too with problems of health and a deepening loneliness. But seemingly the most insistent worry is housing—adequate for dignity and self-respect and adequate too for the deep-felt longings to carry on in life."

SHE BEGAN SCOUTING possible locations. On October 13, 1953, her travels brought her to the lovely little town of Ojai, in a bucolic setting some 80 miles northwest of Los Angeles in Ventura County. She was there to talk with teachers at the local high school. During her visit, someone drew her attention to the defunct Grey Gables Inn, which was up for sale.

In Grey Gables, Dr. Andrus found the property she was looking for. But before she could buy it, she had to win over city officials, who were considering at least two rival bidders—Alcoholics Anonymous and "a resort of uncertain moral standards."

"Finally, at long last," Dr. Andrus wrote, "the City Council felt our institution would be the least worst."

Even with the city's reluctant support, Dr. Andrus faced another challenge: The fledgling NRTA did not have enough cash on hand for a down payment. It looked as though

MEMBER SURVEYS

Dr. Andrus often asked members about potential programs and services that would best suit their needs. Topics included:

Housing Whether NRTA should build a residence for active retired teachers (which led to the establishment of Grey Gables, in Ojai, California)

Travel Interest in affordable group tours to Europe and other destinations (which launched in 1958)

Drug discounts Group savings on popular medicines (which were offered in 1959)

Health, living conditions and employment Tallied for the 1961 White House Conference on Aging

this Ojai opportunity would slip away. Then, in a remarkable twist of fate, Dr. Andrus was rescued by a connection she had forged decades earlier, during her days at Hull House in Chicago.

Kate Crane Gartz had been an activist who served at Hull House with Dr. Andrus. Her daughter, Gloria Gartz, was a retired teacher who had served under Dr. Andrus at Lincoln High School. And Kate Gartz's father, Richard T. Crane, had been a wealthy industrialist and a major financial backer of Hull House. Part of his fortune eventually reached his granddaughter Gloria, who in the spring of 1954 put up $75,000 to guarantee the loan that enabled NRTA to acquire Grey Gables. In September, Grey Gables reopened as the first national retirement home for teachers.

Like Hull House in its day, Grey Gables was an experiment in communal living. Dr. Andrus and Ruth Lana moved to Ojai to take personal charge of the project. (At the same time, Grey Gables became NRTA's new national headquarters.) Dr. Andrus was pioneering a new model of retirement for America. Retirees would not be warehoused until they died. They would live in comfort and be encouraged to engage with the world, in part by continu-

Dr. Andrus reviews the blueprints for Grey Gables.

ing to serve younger people as volunteer teachers and mentors. This was a carryover from Dr. Andrus' Lincoln High School days, when she had emphasized extracurricular activities and encouraged her students to volunteer in the community. Now she prescribed the same formula to Grey Gables residents, with similarly beneficial results.

"We of Grey Gables are certain that this project will be a pilot one, the first perhaps of many to prove to the world that retirement can prove to be a dynamic adventure in gracious living," she wrote in the *NRTA Journal* in September 1954 as she prepared to open its doors.

By that point, Grey Gables had acquired its first tenant, Emma M. Turner, the Andrus sisters' old friend from Chicago, who had arrived in July. By Christmas, eight other former teachers had joined her, and some already were mentoring in schools in the surrounding Ojai community. Local officials were now happy that their "least worst" option for the property was working out. Dr. Andrus' Grey Gables would prove an asset to Ojai in many ways—including financially, as the steady growth of NRTA created local job opportunities for office workers at the new headquarters.

ARTIST RENDERING OF GREY GABLES, A RETIREMENT COMMUNITY AS WELL AS HEADQUARTERS FOR THE NATIONAL RETIRED TEACHERS ASSOCIATION

CLUB-STYLE LIVING THE GREY GABLES VAN TAKES RESIDENTS TO RUN ERRANDS AND ON DAY TRIPS.

GREY GABLES

Clockwise from top left: Residents are served three wholesome meals a day in the communal dining room. Shuffleboard is a popular outdoor activity. Residents socialize on the porch. Santa Claus and his reindeer fly over the roof in the warm California winter.

Teacher at Heart

E THEL PERCY ANDRUS was a woman on a mission. She was making no little plans—to echo Chicago architect Daniel Burnham's words. She was determined to harness the latent power of her peers—the thousands of teachers who had devoted four or five decades of their lives to their profession and were now forced to abandon their classrooms when they still had much to contribute. Dr. Andrus had a job for them. As they had once educated their students, these dedicated teachers would, by their example, educate their fellow retirees, the many millions of older Americans who were being forced into obsolescence by mandatory retirement.

"As it is," she told *Time* magazine in 1954, "when you leave a job, they often just give you a gold watch, and all you can do is look at it and count the hours until you die. Yet think of all the grand things we can do that youth can't. Think of all the things we already have done."

And think of all the things they could do in the future. People were living longer than previous generations, which meant that a teacher who retired at 65 might have 10 or more years of active life. What would she do with herself? Dr. Andrus had some suggestions: "We don't get old—we grow old—we mature. If we ever stop growing, then we've had it."

Dr. Andrus and her peers—what she called a pilot generation—would create a new template for people 65 and older. She emphasized "the value we place on the individuality of each of us, a person with hopes, aspirations and capacities. ... We hope the picture to be considered a typical one will present us facing confidently an entirely new present and an unknown future—our problem, a highly individualized one and a social one as well, trying to continue in the full stream of life."

In April 1954, Dr. Andrus was named National Teacher of the Year by the National Education Association, the National Congress of Parents and Teachers, and her own NRTA. The citation mentioned her tireless efforts

'Children of 1954 Know More'

'Teacher of Year' Has Two Devotions

Examiner Apr 18, 1954

Lauds Youth; Aids Retirees' Homes

Children of all ages—their "growing-up" years often the brunt of criticism by adults—yesterday found a champion in a former teacher and principal of Los Angeles schools.

Dr. Ethel Percy Andrus, 28 years principal of Abraham Lincoln High School, and now president of the National Retired Teachers' association, declared:

"I think children today are more fun-loving, more natural, more adept at tackling responsibilities. They are a long ways from going 'to seed' as some experts want us to believe."

The quiet-spoken educator, who admits she is not adverse to using slang phrases of youth herself, went even further:

"Children today certainly know more than we did in our youth. They have a greater vocabulary, a fuller knowledge of world affairs. And, it hasn't done them a bit of harm."

'TEACHER OF YEAR'—

The 71-year-old woman, who says she believes in "not growing old," has just been named National Teacher of the Year, for her work in directing fundraising drives for the building of retired teachers' homes throughout the country. She went on:

"The challenge is to give children responsibilities during their 'growing

ert Preston, Robert Young, Frank Jenks and John Doucette, TV villain "who knocks them cold in every reel" she says; and George Smith, present principal of Lincoln High.

Yesterday, she said, "I truthfully do not have any special memories—because all of those years (some 40 to be more explicit) were so grand. I relish them all."

HER AMBITION

Besides her "children," Dr. Andrus dreams only of the day when she will have established the National Retired Teachers' Home in Ojai, on the Grey Gables estate.

The Home is expected to be in operation by late June, and in time will accommodate 80 persons—all retired teachers who will participate in a well-rounded program of activities to keep them "young in heart."

"Young man, the tragedy of old age is inactivity," Dr.

1954

DR. ANDRUS IS NAMED NATIONAL TEACHER OF THE YEAR, RECEIVING THE HONOR AT LINCOLN HIGH SCHOOL.

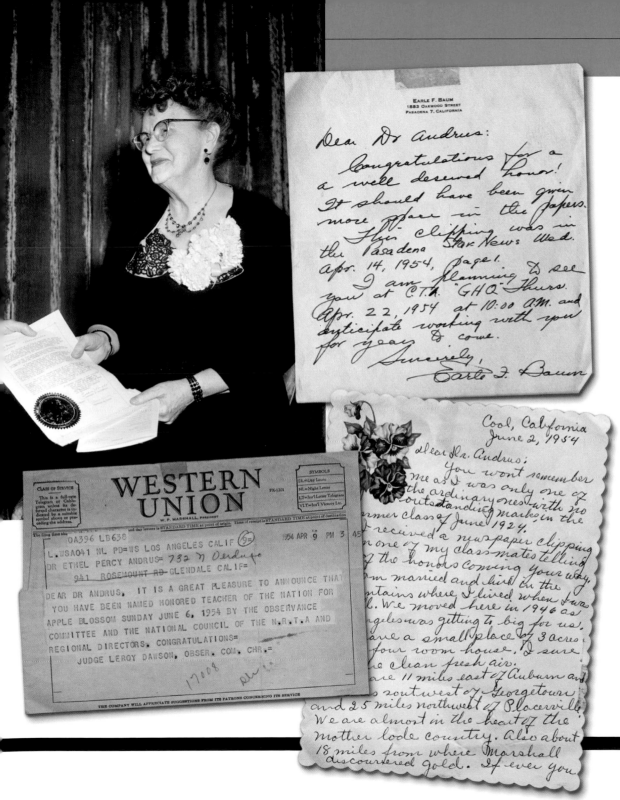

to raise funds for teacher retirement homes, including the new one in Ojai. She received her award in June, in a ceremony at Lincoln High School with many of her former students—including California Governor Goodwin Knight—on hand.

Naturally, Dr. Andrus seized the opportunity to publicize Grey Gables. When her award was announced, a *Los Angeles Examiner* reporter noted in his story that the new Ojai facility would accommodate 80 retired teachers "who will participate in a well-rounded program of activities to keep them 'young in heart.'"

"Young man, the tragedy of old age is inactivity. We hope to prevent this at [Grey Gables]," Dr. Andrus told him. "Never take to the rocking chair when you get on in years. If you do, you are a goner."

Dr. Andrus urged her peers to be adventurous and daring, trying new things and savoring the joys of the present without fear of the future. As a believer in community living, Dr. Andrus wrote of the NRTA residence: Grey Gables "is not an old folks' home, nor is it a rest asylum. It is a vital, delightful home for the creation of new days, new futures and the expansion of old enthusiasms. ... Enjoy yourself. Build a new life *now*. It may be later than you think. It may even be later than you ever thought it could be!"

When Grey Gables opened, in the fall, Dr. Andrus and her NRTA colleagues could congratulate themselves on the success of the group's first seven years. They had boosted teachers' pensions, in effect, by prodding Congress to pass the income-tax exemption. They had fended off efforts to mandate Social Security for teachers in preexisting pension systems. And Grey Gables, with its communal living and its emphasis on volunteerism, was reducing isolation and helping retirees feel useful again.

But a major goal remained out of reach. Despite considerable effort, Dr. Andrus hadn't found an insurance company that would take on the risk of insuring retirees.

CHAPTER 4

"THEY THOUGHT I WAS A

The *NRTA Journal* announcing Dr. Andrus' groundbreaking health insurance plan

Pioneering group health insurance

CRANK"

A **LOT OF COMPANIES** in the United States offered health insurance in the early 1950s, but none were willing to write an affordable health policy for people 65 and over. "Health insurance coverage was denied to older folk," Dr. Ethel Percy Andrus later explained, "or, if coverage was permitted to continue after the age of 60 or 65, the premiums were excessively high, as well as benefits unnecessarily restricted."

That, Dr. Andrus believed, must change. One by one, over a five-year period, she asked 42 companies about setting up coverage for members of the National Retired Teachers Association. She struck out with all 42.

"They thought I was a crank," she recalled, "especially when I told them I wanted a noncancelable, budget-priced group policy ... to be paid for by the month and with no physical examination. Some wouldn't see me; others showed me tables to prove they'd go broke if they wrote the policy I wanted."

This was perhaps not surprising, given that the insurance companies focused on the worst-case scenario: old people in declining health who landed in hospitals.

"Their data came from studies based on people in veterans hospitals," Dr. Andrus said. "'But I've never been in a hospital,' I told them. 'Your trouble is that you don't meet healthy people.'"

Rebuffed again and again, she nonetheless persevered. Her efforts finally made an impression on Robert Decormier, a retired industrial arts teacher from Poughkeepsie, New York. Decormier was both president of the New York State Retired Teachers Association and a vice president of NRTA. He, like Dr. Andrus, was eager to make health insurance available to his members. It was through Decormier that Dr. Andrus finally found an insurance agent willing to take a chance on offering a plan to America's retirees.

On November 2, 1954, Decormier had a fateful encounter with Leonard Davis, an insurance agent for the Continental Casualty Company. It was Election Day, and Decormier had gone to the Hooker Avenue firehouse in Poughkeepsie to cast his ballot. While there, he fell into a conversation with Davis, a local committeeman for that election district.

Davis was born in New York in 1924 and grew up in the Bronx, where his widowed mother ran a candy store. He attended the City College of New York and went into accounting before becoming an insurance broker in Poughkeepsie. He had met Decormier on an earlier occasion, and the two had talked about politics. But on that November day, Decormier had something else on his mind.

Davis recalled the conversation years later: "It was after [Decormier] had voted that he started to speak to me and my co-committeeperson, who was also in the insurance business, about the problems he had with his retired teachers in the state of New York. And my co-committeeperson said, well, he was sorry that there was nothing he could think that he or anybody could do for him."

But Davis had a different reaction. One of his clients, Atlantic City Electric Company, had recently arranged with Continental Casualty for a group medical plan that also covered the company's retirees. As a result, Davis had been accumulating data about covering older people—data that few other people were compiling in the mid-1950s.

Ethel Says

"I was convinced that the insurance industry held false and immature fears of aging."

"Throughout the United States, and particularly in the public educational systems, when people needed insurance the most, they were automatically being canceled when they retired at age 65," Davis said. "Atlantic City Electric Company was one of the few exceptions that still cared about their retired people and decided to keep them on as part of their group policy."

Of course, writing a policy for all of New York's retired teachers would be a much bigger endeavor. Davis asked Decormier how much of a premium he thought his members could pay.

"He said they could afford $5 a month," Davis said. "And then I said to the insurance company, 'How much insurance can we offer for $5 a month?'"

The answer: enough to make the experiment worthwhile. This would be a pilot program, to see whether Continental Casualty could profitably insure a large group of retirees. About 800 of Decormier's roughly 5,000 New York members signed up for the plan, which required no physical examination. The project was tested early on when an influenza outbreak threatened to swamp the system with overwhelming costs. But most of Decormier's New York teachers fended off the flu bug, offering insurers hope that they could cover retirees without going broke.

Decormier relayed the exciting news to Dr. Andrus, who asked him to bring Davis to NRTA's 1955 national convention in Chicago, where Dr. Andrus had started her career at the Lewis Institute half a century earlier.

"She was a woman that would be very hard to describe," Davis said of Dr. Andrus, who was now in her mid-70s. "She was a very, very exciting person to be with. To be in her presence was a wonderful experience. To see her work was an unusual experience. And, most important, to see her commitment to people, her selfless commitment to people, was something that was remarkable."

For Dr. Andrus, meeting Davis would become the turning point in her long quest. Here was an insurance

QUEST FOR COVERAGE

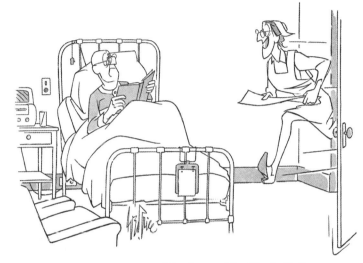

"*Good news, Mr. Murdock! You can go home as soon as you fork over $593.50.*"

man willing to take a chance on covering older people. She had to make this work.

"If you could do it for New York state," she asked Davis, "could you do it for the National Retired Teachers Association, as well?"

Davis wasn't sure. At that point, the New York pilot program "was just borderline successful," he recalled. By covering a vastly larger group of retirees, Continental Casualty might be putting itself in jeopardy. He offered Dr. Andrus a less comprehensive policy for the same premium. She turned it down and went home to California disappointed.

"Where Can We Get Insurance?" read the headline in the June 1954 *NRTA Journal*. The article outlined the quest for affordable health insurance for retired people.

"To our knowledge, there is no health insurance or medical insurance plan which begins to meet the health contingencies of old age; and some of them disqualify a person for membership once he has reached the age of 65 or has retired," the article stated. "If there were such a plan, it is obvious that it would be much more costly than current plans, and probably too costly to be financed from the reduced income of most retired persons.

"Most self-respecting retirees would consider medical charity acceptable only as a last resort. It seems to us inevitable then that there must be developed a prepaid health insurance or medical service plan which will include the major health contingencies of retirement."

Thanks to the determination of Dr. Andrus and the vision of Robert Decormier, president of the New York State Retired Teachers Association, this dream became reality.

Four years later, she would quip, "The need was acknowledged. It was like the weather: Everyone talkin'; nobody doin'."

A Radical Plan

BUT THEN Leonard Davis came back to Dr. Andrus with an offer that she could agree to. "A goal achieved," she announced in the September 1955 *NRTA Journal*. At long last, NRTA members would have access to an affordable insurance plan that paid specific amounts for hospitalization, outpatient hospital care, medical care in the hospital and surgery.

Taking the New York plan nationwide was not yet a done deal. There were still details to be worked out—unforeseen snags and last-minute renegotiations. The work absorbed a tremendous amount of Dr. Andrus' time and energy, as she conceded ruefully in the June 1956 *NRTA Journal*. At last, however, she had a workable health plan to present to her members.

"We commend it to you as the very best noncancelable coverage that you can secure in retirement without limitation on age or physical examination to determine preexisting condition of applicants for admission," she wrote. "The chief actuary of the Continental Casualty Company, underwriters of the policy, expresses the view that the company and the NRTA in this project are 'fostering a new milestone in the progress of retired people.'"

That milestone was reached on July 1, when the historic NRTA plan took effect—the first nationwide health plan for a large group of retired people.

"I suggested to Dr. Andrus that if we were going to institute this program, that it best be handled out of Washington, D.C.," Davis recalled. "I further suggested to

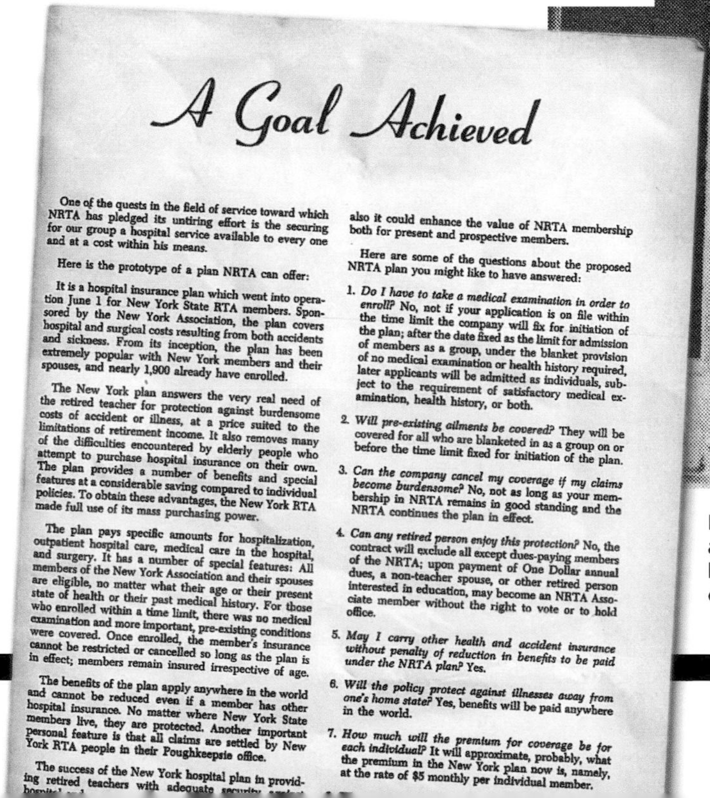

A Goal Achieved

One of the quests in the field of service toward which NRTA has pledged its untiring effort is the securing for our group a hospital service available to every one and at a cost within his means.

Here is the prototype of a plan NRTA can offer:

It is a hospital insurance plan which went into operation June 1 for New York State RTA members. Sponsored by the New York Association, the plan covers hospital and surgical costs resulting from both accidents and sickness. From its inception, the plan has been extremely popular with New York members and their spouses, and nearly 1,900 already have enrolled.

The New York plan answers the very real need of the retired teacher for protection against burdensome costs of accident or illness, at a price suited to the limitations of retirement income. It also removes many of the difficulties encountered by elderly people who attempt to purchase hospital insurance on their own. The plan provides a number of benefits and special features at a considerable saving compared to individual policies. To obtain these advantages, the New York RTA made full use of its mass purchasing power.

The plan pays specific amounts for hospitalization, outpatient hospital care, medical care in the hospital, and surgery. It has a number of special features: All members of the New York Association and their spouses are eligible, no matter what their age or their present state of health or their past medical history. For those who enrolled within a time limit, there was no medical examination and more important, pre-existing conditions were covered. Once enrolled, the member's insurance cannot be restricted or cancelled so long as the plan is in effect; members remain insured irrespective of age.

The benefits of the plan apply anywhere in the world and cannot be reduced even if a member has other hospital insurance. No matter where New York State members live, they are protected. Another important personal feature is that all claims are settled by New York RTA people in their Poughkeepsie office.

The success of the New York hospital plan in providing retired teachers with adequate

also it could enhance the value of NRTA membership both for present and prospective members.

Here are some of the questions about the proposed NRTA plan you might like to have answered:

1. *Do I have to take a medical examination in order to enroll?* No, not if your application is on file within the time limit the company will fix for initiation of the plan; after the date fixed as the limit for admission of members as a group, under the blanket provision of no medical examination or health history required, later applicants will be admitted as individuals, subject to the requirement of satisfactory medical examination, health history, or both.

2. *Will pre-existing ailments be covered?* They will be covered for all who are blanketed in as a group on or before the time limit fixed for initiation of the plan.

3. *Can the company cancel my coverage if my claims become burdensome?* No, not as long as your membership in NRTA remains in good standing and the NRTA continues the plan in effect.

4. *Can any retired person enjoy this protection?* No, the contract will exclude all except dues-paying members of the NRTA; upon payment of One Dollar annual dues, a non-teacher spouse, or other retired person interested in education, may become an NRTA Associate member without the right to vote or to hold office.

5. *May I carry other health and accident insurance without penalty of reduction in benefits to be paid under the NRTA plan?* Yes.

6. *Will the policy protect against illnesses away from one's home state?* Yes, benefits will be paid anywhere in the world.

7. *How much will the premium for coverage be for each individual?* It will approximate, probably, what the premium in the New York plan now is, namely, at the rate of $5 monthly per individual member.

Left: Dr. Andrus and her staff review a flood of mail about the group health plan. Above: Headquarters of the insurance plan in Washington

TYPICAL MONTHLY FAMILY EXPENSES IN 1950

Average income: $353

HEALTH CARE	$16
APPAREL	$36
TRANSPORTATION	$43
HOUSING	$86
FOOD	$94
OTHER	$70

herself in the nation's capital, a place that would come to know her well.

In the plan's first year, 5,000 NRTA members signed up for policies. Dr. Andrus had delivered the goods for her members. She never looked back. Later, in 1957 and 1958, NRTA began offering a new option, Plan A, which provided greatly increased hospital benefits plus medical calls in the hospital for a slightly higher premium. (The original plan was now designated Plan B.) July 1959 brought another innovation: a postoperative nursing home benefit.

Although Leonard Davis was instrumental in this process, he always saluted Dr. Andrus as the catalyst. It was "under the inspired leadership of our great national president, Dr. Andrus, that our great organization, the National Retired Teachers Association, took this pioneering concept of health insurance for older persons and brought it to what we have today—the plan that broke the barriers against health insurance for retired teachers and led to a new era for all older persons," Davis said. "Now that the practicality of health insurance for the aged is universally accepted, it seems difficult to realize that only a few short years ago, those of us who believed in it were considered visionaries."

Meanwhile, NRTA had achieved milestones beyond health insurance. In September 1955, in the same *NRTA Journal* issue that trumpeted the new health coverage, Dr. Andrus took stock of her eight-year-old organization.

"Today we are more than 20,000 strong," she wrote. "Our organization extends from Maine to Florida, from Alaska to Hawaii. We are publishers of a journal, now in its 23rd issue. We own a retirement residence of real beauty, quality and comfort, licensed to accommodate 49 members without counting our new additions. We are again part of the national educational picture, and we have attained a major legislative victory. All this has come about because of our positive attitude toward life, unafraid of the challenging future."

her that in order for her to be comfortable, I would like her to designate somebody from her organization in whom she had a lot of trust to be involved in the administration of the program."

Dr. Andrus tapped her longtime friend and fellow Grey Gables resident Grace Hatfield, who moved from Ojai to Washington to serve as NRTA's insurance coordinator. Thus did Dr. Ethel Percy Andrus first establish

← **$5 A MONTH** THE PREMIUM COVERED EMERGENCY CARE, HOSPITAL ROOM, SURGERY AND MORE.

"We must strive in all areas of life to strengthen American democracy."

—ETHEL PERCY ANDRUS

Lighting the Torch

Dr. Andrus, talking with residents of Grey Gables

O**N A PERSONAL LEVEL,** after four decades in Glendale, California, Dr. Andrus was now happily settled in Ojai, at Grey Gables, which she had designed as a showcase for active NRTA members, to show the world what they could achieve when properly supported and motivated.

"Grey Gables is definitely not either a rest home nor an old folks home," Dr. Andrus wrote. "It is a place for teachers no longer in active service who can make of retirement fulfillment rather than escape. For this reason we are seeking for this experiment teachers with adventurous good will who are forward looking and who believe that the future holds for them an adventure in the fine art of living together for the common good. We urge upon our prospective candidates that the time to begin in a new career in living is when one sees life as still enriching and enlarging. To wait until one has exhausted the possibilities of enjoyment is to wait too long; Grey Gables is not for them."

Although single all her life, Dr. Andrus had never lived alone. She resided with her parents and then her mother, nursing her back to health after retiring from Lincoln High School. Following her mother's death in 1951, Dr. Andrus continued to share a Glendale house with Ruth Lana and Lana's daughter, Lora, until 1954, when all three moved to Grey Gables. So did Dr. Andrus' sister, Maud; Maud's son, Lincoln Andrus Service, a physician who provided medical care for Gables residents; and his two young daughters, Barbara and Suzanne, bringing to five the number of Andrus family members in Ojai.

"We just loved Ojai," Barbara Service recalled. "It was rural and very beautiful."

But Dr. Andrus' idea of family embraced a wider circle than her blood kin, her longtime personal secretary, Virginia Schott, later noted.

"When she was just a little girl, she knew she wanted to accomplish a lot in the world," Schott remembered. "She said that her father had told her that she must never marry if she wanted to achieve the goals she had in mind. That's why she didn't marry. But she had a different

> "We just loved Ojai. It was rural and very beautiful."
>
> –Barbara Service, Dr. Andrus' grandniece (Maud's grandchild)

kind of family—all of her students, everyone she worked with—they were her family."

From the quiet enclave of Ojai, Dr. Andrus shared her philosophy and ideas through the pages of the *NRTA Journal.* She was attentive to what others wrote, too. The *NRTA Journal* was not the only publication geared to the interests of America's burgeoning retirees. For example, the *Journal of Lifetime Living* ran an article in June 1955 that caught her eye. The author was the well-known radio journalist H.V. Kaltenborn, who at 76 was focusing on issues that concerned his contemporaries. The headline posed a question: "Should We Seniors Form a Union?"In response, Dr. Andrus reminded her readers that NRTA already had a strong organization that sought to benefit older Americans—but not at the expense of the young.

In the September issue of the *NRTA Journal,* she wrote: "He says, 'If we were to become merely a selfish and narrow instrument for securing federal handouts, it would be a treacherous thing,' and then he suggests the kind of serviceable and dedicated program that NRTA has proudly adopted—the correction of abuses, without the blight of selfish class services. We have utilized our riper experience and our greater leisure and our informed leadership in the interest of all retired folk. There are still inequities to be removed. There is still unfinished legislative business to be followed through."

Dr. Andrus was clearly broadening her activist horizons. Many NRTA members had, like Andrus, entered the profession during the heady days of the Progressive Era. Five decades later, their hair might be turning gray, but they had lost little of their enthusiasm. These were old friends and former colleagues. They still had energy and idealism to burn, plus the added benefit of a lifetime of experience to guide them.

"All our professional lives, as teachers, we have fought the good fight—the eternal fight between good and evil, between inertia and purpose, between apathy and the growth of social concern," Dr. Andrus wrote. "All our professional years we have seriously accepted these responsibilities.

CHUCKLES

MOST *NRTA JOURNAL* ISSUES ENDED WITH JOKES. THESE ARE FROM 1954 AND 1955.

The little boy peered over the edge of the stationery counter at the ten-cent store and asked hopefully, "Have you got any blank report cards?"

Father: "Don't you think Junior got his intelligence from me?" Mother: "He must have. I still have mine."

The teacher had been instructing her first graders in the alphabet. "Peter," she asked, "what letter comes after 'A'?" Peter thought for a moment, then brightened. "All of them?"

The only things that children wear out faster than shoes are parents and teachers.

"As retired folk, we find ourselves somehow relieved of the heavy tangible pressures involved in our former work. We are told that we have earned the right to rest and, without limitations, to play the role we like in advancing our own interests. As no other segment in America's adult population, we retired folk have leisure, that precious treasure of free time that grants us the opportunity for such personal satisfaction and for our own meaningful growth."

But leisure and growth came with additional responsibility. "As retired folk," Dr. Andrus continued, "we recognize these personal advantages but, as educators, we know that we must go on utilizing these advantages in doing our share in creating in our communities an affirmative climate of opinion, to the best of our ability helping our communities build toward more beauty, less prejudice, better schools and a more sustained sense of public responsibility.

" ... Let us show to the world about us the truth that Plato once said, 'Those having torches will pass them on to others.' May our torches of enthusiasm and dedication help others play a vital role in the American drama of today, a day when America needs its creative leaders, needs again to put to work its social innovators."

As retired educators, they had fought to improve the lives of their fellow retired teachers. What about the millions of retirees who hadn't been teachers, who had no NRTA to fight for them? Dr. Andrus saw an opening, something that could only be described by her favorite word—that word emblazoned on Lincoln High School's gate: "opportunity."

The NRTA insurance program had created that opening. Once NRTA proved the plan was feasible for retired teachers, Continental Casualty offered similar coverage to members of the National Association of Retired Civil Employees. Meanwhile, retirees who didn't belong to those groups were asking Dr. Andrus why they couldn't sign up, too. The next challenge was obvious: What if Dr. Andrus formed a new group, one that any retiree could join?

CHAPTER 5

"A REAL AND THR CHAL

Dr. Andrus' collaborations strengthened her work. Here she meets with American Red Cross and YWCA representatives.

Members sailed aboard the gracious *Queen Elizabeth* in the summer of 1958.

ILLING ENGE"

AARP: Independence, dignity, purpose

MEMBERSHIP IN THE National Retired Teachers Association surged in 1957, thanks to the popularity of the organization's new health plan. This prompted a question: How could Dr. Ethel Percy Andrus help retirees who were not eligible to join NRTA but still needed health insurance? Near the end of the year, she called Leonard Davis, the insurance broker who had set up the initial plan.

"She said, 'Now that we have proven this so successful, I have been getting some people who are not teachers asking me if we could do some of the things that we're doing for the retired teachers for the general retired people,'" Davis recalled. "At that point she said, 'I'm thinking of setting up an organization in the state of California for ... just retired people,' and she asked what I thought about it. I replied that I thought the idea had a lot of merit but asked her why confine it to the state of California? I told her that if she was going to get involved with such a venture, why not think about doing it on a nationwide basis? She replied, 'Well, I'd like to think about that.'"

Dr. Andrus consulted some longtime allies. Those who urged caution included Robert Decormier, the New York State Retired Teachers Association leader who helped create NRTA's pioneering group insurance offering, and Lila Armstrong, who taught at Lincoln High School when Dr. Andrus was principal. Both thought Dr. Andrus already had enough on her plate with NRTA.

"If Dr. Andrus had listened to me, she never would have started AARP," Armstrong said years later.

The doubters felt that America's retirees would never coalesce into a cohesive group. They had nothing in common except being retired and over 65. What would bring them together? Dr. Andrus saw it: the promise of health insurance and the idea that life didn't end at 65.

NRTA was beginning to grow, with Grace Hatfield in Washington, D.C., administering the new insurance program, and Ruth Lana traveling frequently to New York, coordinating its new travel agency. The organization remained headquartered at Grey Gables in Ojai, but Dr. Andrus now spent much of her time in Washington. And it was there, at the Woodner apartments, that the American Association of Retired Persons began to take shape.

The date was April 30, 1958. Three people were present: Dr. Andrus, Grace Hatfield and Ernest Giddings, a lobbyist for the National Education Association, with which NRTA was associated. They resolved to create an organization allied to NRTA but independent of it.

A follow-up meeting was held in California, a month or so later. Six people convened for dinner at the Ojai Valley Inn, which was a favorite weekend getaway for Hollywood celebrities. Those at the table: Dr. Andrus; Ruth Lana; Leonard Davis; Davis' insurance associate, Leonard Fialkow; Dr. Andrus' first cousin Dorothy Crippen, who had recently retired as a teacher in Palo Alto, California, to join the NRTA team in Ojai; and Dr. Andrus' Ojai attorney, Jack Fay.

Dr. Andrus announced her decision to start a new national organization, open to every American over the age of 55 who paid membership dues of $2 per year.

"They had a terrible time deciding how to name the [organization]," Lana later recollected. "[Dr. Andrus] didn't like the word 'people.'" She sought to showcase members as zestful, energetic individuals—not as an undifferentiated mass of retired people.

"And she didn't like 'senior citizen,'" continued Lana. "She also wanted to be as far up on the alphabet as possible, so when you opened the phone book, there we'd be. And so we tried American Association. We got that," Lana said. They couldn't get a third 'A', so "we went with Retired Persons."

These two small meetings laid the groundwork for an enormous success, bigger than anyone at the meet-

AARP's Inception

APRIL 1958
Dr. Andrus lays plans for AARP during a meeting at her apartment at the Woodner (above) in Washington, D.C., with two trusted allies: Grace Hatfield (NRTA insurance coordinator) and Ernest Giddings (associate legislative director for the National Education Association).

1957
The idea for a new organization is sparked by hundreds of letters from noneducators seeking affordable health insurance.

ings envisioned. As the dinner meeting broke up, Fay recalled, Davis took him aside and whispered in his ear, "You'll never get anywhere in life if you don't think big!"

This comment echoed the words attributed to the architect Daniel Burnham, presiding genius of Chicago's World's Fair of 1893: "Make no little plans!" Dr. Andrus had taken that advice to heart when she founded NRTA. Now she was rolling the dice again.

Incorporated on July 1, the American Association of Retired Persons described itself in its magazine as "a nonprofit organization made up of a great number of persons, mature in age and outlook, who hopefully believe that together they can help build a better future for themselves and for others of their generation."

As Dr. Andrus once said: "We know in us, retired folk, are planted powers more than sufficient to our needs; we possess resourcefulness and courage of maturity. Realizing this potential strength we felt it to be our solemn obligation to unite in service and with faith for the betterment of … our people."

LATE SPRING 1958
Plans are refined over dinner at the Ojai Valley Inn in California.

1958
Member dues at AARP's inception are $2 a year.

Ethel Says
"Why is there such a stigma attached to old age? We love old wines, old laces, old masters— why not old people?"

JULY 1, 1958
AARP is founded when its certificate of incorporation is filed in Washington, D.C.

OCTOBER 1958
The first issue of *Modern Maturity* magazine is published.

JULY 1960
A new legal seal—featuring an eagle and "Independence, Purpose, Dignity"—is approved by the AARP Board of Directors.

MODERN MATURITY

Chat With The Editor

Ethelwyn Andrus

Sometimes you get to thinking that your problems are peculiar to you and just can't be solved. Well, perhaps they are, but, eleven years ago some retired teachers discovered that they worried about the same things, and so they started to see what they could do in finding, if not a solution, at least a semi-solution.

They banded together and formed a National Retired Teachers Association, which now has a membership of 100,000. They began the publication of a journal, which has not only earned the honor of being quoted in national magazines but has generated in its membership the warmth of a sense of togetherness. They have successfully pioneered in securing for themselves and their spouses, at a budget price, health and hospital insurance coverage, without either evidence of insurability or age restriction or right of cancellation by the insurance company as long as the master contract remains in force.

This achievement the United States Department of Health, Education and Welfare has highly complimented. The Continental Casualty Company, under which the insurance policies are written, names it as a "major contribution to the solution of one of the most urgent problems facing our country today." Then, not content with providing hospitalization coverage, they again pioneered in gaining group rates for their people in travel, with the assurance of fixed prices, a leisurely-paced program, an informed guide continuously serving the group.

Perhaps the benefits they have gained themselves may be the answer to some needs. Perhaps we retired persons other teachers too feel the need to have a place in society, to have a respected place in the eyes of others, to be doing something that is interesting and significant in our own to have a national voice. We believe th...

National Retired Teachers Association has realized for its membership these goals.

And so, modeling ourselves upon their pattern, with their encouragement, approval and support, we contacted the insurance and travel companies, and we secured for you similar insurance and travel advantages. We asked and gained the endorsement of the United States Department of Health, Education and Welfare for an organization of retired persons, with its own publication and its own program of welfare.

The National Association of Retired Persons is a voluntary group pledged to find for its members the maximum of common interests, to invite all older folk to take an active role in meeting resourcefully the needs of all phases of the lengthening life span. MODERN MATURITY in this endeavor hopes to be a friendly medium of exchange and good fellowship.

We know we will all be better off for it.

Aging is not just a problem; it represents a real and thrilling challenge. It is one thing to recognize that older people represent the nation's greatest single human resource available and it is quite another to do something about it.

Oct.-Nov. 1958

MODERN MATURITY

Vol. 1, No. 1

MODERN MATURITY is published every other month by American Association of Retired Persons as a service to its membership.
It is not sold on newsstands

Promoting a New Image of Aging

B **ACK HOME IN OJAI,** Dr. Andrus began roughing out plans for a magazine that would serve the social and cultural needs of AARP members. It would provide a new image of aging, exploring common challenges and sharing stories of men and women who continued to strive, grow and enjoy life as they matured.

Leonard Davis and his family were vacationing in Anaheim at Disneyland in the summer of 1958 when Dr. Andrus called from Ojai, a two-hour drive to the north.

"I'd like to come down and show you something," she said to him.

The "something" was a mockup of the first issue of *Modern Maturity*. The new magazine was so crucial to the successful launch of AARP that Davis cut short his Disneyland trip and drove up to Grey Gables to spend

Readers found job tips, inspiration and a modern view of aging in AARP's magazine.

← THE FIRST ISSUE OF AARP'S *MODERN MATURITY* WAS PUBLISHED IN OCTOBER 1958.

63

JUNE 27, 1959
DR. ANDRUS (FAR LEFT) AT THE FIRST AARP BOARD OF DIRECTORS MEETING. WITH BACKGROUNDS IN GOVERNMENT, COMMUNITY AFFAIRS AND EDUCATION, MEMBERS OF THE FIRST BOARD ALSO INCLUDED PEOPLE CLOSE TO DR. ANDRUS. HERE ARE A FEW OF THEM.

RUTH LANA
Retired math teacher, director of NRTA Travel Service, AARP executive secretary

MAUD ANDRUS SERVICE
Ethel's older sister, former Lincoln High School teacher, who assisted with NRTA-AARP publications

DOROTHY CRIPPEN
Dr. Andrus' first cousin, trusted adviser and NRTA-AARP executive

LINCOLN SERVICE, M.D.
Nephew of Dr. Andrus, physician for Grey Gables and Acacia residents, in Ojai, California; later an AARP drug consultant

ALICE REITERMAN
Retired math teacher; close friend of Dr. Andrus; NRTA Financial Secretary

a few days perfecting the mockup with Dr. Andrus, her sister Maud and Ruth Lana.

The first issue of the new bimonthly was dated October-November 1958. It would have been the September-October issue except that Dr. Andrus thought the pastel pinks and blues on the proposed cover wouldn't appeal to prospective male members. Eventually, she selected a photo of trees in full autumn color, appealing to both women and men. The magazine needed to make a good first impression, she knew. It had to captivate readers with compelling articles and high-quality design, starting with the cover. "As you read this first issue of *Modern Maturity,* we hope you will find many interesting features which will relax or stimulate you according to your moods," she told her readers.

And Dr. Andrus concluded by disrupting stereotypical views of getting older: "Aging is not just a problem; it represents a real and thrilling challenge. It is one thing to recognize that older people represent the nation's greatest single human resource available and it is quite another to do something about it."

That first issue went to the entire NRTA membership, inviting them to sign up for AARP and to recommend the new organization to their friends. Articles discussed a range of topics. How-tos covered finding a job despite being over 65, keeping fit ("How a Queen Stays Slim") and becoming a better bridge player. There were book reviews and an article on aging by Eleanor Roosevelt. The first issue made a prominent pitch for the AARP group insurance plan, which took up five of the magazine's 52 pages.

The magazine proclaimed its ambitions and high purpose from the outset: "to create a showcase for the achievement of our people; to build many bridges between the worlds of our needs and the powers that can answer those needs; to open the door to all the various human adventures we can picture for you; and to serve as a forum for the discussion of subjects of interest to retired persons."

From that first issue of *Modern Maturity,* Dr. Andrus sent readers a clear message: Being older was not a disability; it was an opportunity.

Expanding Horizons With Group Travel

FROM NEW YORK

ENGLAND

HOLLAND

BELGIUM

GERMANY

FRANCE

SWITZERLAND

ITALY

MONACO

INAUGURAL TRIP ITINERARY

Travelers on the first group tour enjoyed personal service throughout their 45-day visit to Europe. They sailed from New York to Great Britain, then went to six other countries before sailing home—all for $895.

4 DAYS London, Stratford, Oxford, Windsor
1 DAY Holland and the Hague

2 DAYS Brussels
3 DAYS Germany
3 DAYS Switzerland
9 DAYS Italy

3 DAYS Italian Riviera and the principality of Monaco
4 DAYS Paris

MANY RETIREES wanted to see Europe—but travel was often too costly and the logistics too difficult to navigate. A new group travel plan developed by NRTA and then AARP soon turned armchair travelers into savvy tourists. It marked the first time that group tours had been designed for older travelers who were not wealthy.

Ruth Lana remembered the birth of the idea. They'd been talking about it in Ojai. How many members had been out of the United States? Why should they just stay at home?

Then, one day, right before the *NRTA Journal* was going to press, Lana later recalled, "All of a sudden, someone said, 'Well, we could do travel. Why don't we find out how many people would be interested?' So Dr. Andrus opened the book and took out one little article. And down at the bottom of a page in one of the magazines, in whichever edition it was, is, 'If you're interested in travel, write.'"

Positive responses prompted Dr. Andrus to launch the travel service, in the spring of 1958. Lana took charge of the new program, which immediately resonated with members.

In the summer of 1958, some 300 members traveled to Europe from New York City in groups of 25. They sailed on majestic ocean liners. (At that time, commercial transatlantic airline flights were still in their infancy.) The package included all lodging, meals, transportation, escorted tours and assistance with luggage for the entire 45-day inaugural tour of England, Holland, Belgium, Germany, Switzerland, Italy, Monaco and France. The price? $895.

"Our returning travelers are our best advertisers," Dr. Andrus wrote a year later, in the *NRTA Journal*. "They have enjoyed the facilities provided for them, the care afforded them and the sights, which but for the rates offered, they might not have been able to enjoy."

1958 THE FIRST TOUR GROUP LEAVES FROM NEW YORK CITY. BELOW: A BOAT RIDE IN SWITZERLAND

ON THE MOON-DRENCHED DECK OF AN OCEAN LINER...

ON A SLEEK-SOARING JET...

OR IN THE COMFORTABLE INTERIOR OF A BUS...

THESE SONGS WILL GIVE A LIFT TO THE NRTA-AARP TRAVELER

Ruth Lana
RUTH LANA
Executive Director, Services

SONGS FOR THE HAPPY TRAVELERS

Dedication ceremony for expanding the Acacias nursing facility: Dr. Andrus with Ralph Bennett, the mayor of Ojai (center), and Richard York, administrator of the Acacias

Healing Body and Spirit

HE NRTA-AARP insurance and travel programs were just the start of Dr. Andrus' market-changing services.

Until the 1950s, older people who were physically or mentally incapacitated had difficulty finding suitable care. Living with family members, residing in special homes run by women's or church groups, or being relegated to poorhouses (sometimes called asylums) were often the only options. Although the number of nursing homes began growing after World War II, few in the 1950s provided skilled nursing services, such as care for recently hospitalized people who were too sick to go home.

Dr. Andrus knew from personal experience that recovery was possible for ailing people in their 80s. Her own mother had recovered her health and enjoyed seven more years of life after Dr. Andrus retired from Lincoln High to care for her. She designed the Acacias—an innovative skilled nursing facility across the street from Grey Gables in Ojai—to care for people as she had done for her mother.

"The Acacias hopes to be more than a nursing facility, more than a convalescent home; it is a health center— the first one, we hope, of many—that will demonstrate

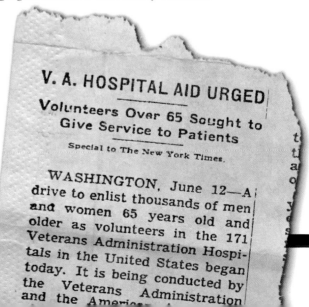

the potency of helping older people discover the basis of their trouble and through care, friendly concern and expert service find the right channels to recovery," she wrote in *Modern Maturity*. "The Acacias in its freshness and beauty of building and setting is in itself a strong factor in the attainment of this goal; its lines are restful; its colors refreshing; its furnishing modern and effective."

The Acacias included private and semiprivate rooms, each with a TV and telephone. In addition to food "rich in vitamins, proteins and minerals as part of our medical therapy," the *NRTA Journal* explained, "provision is planned for easy transition from bed care with supervised bathing to full self-care, as the patient progresses in his convalescence." Together, Grey Gables and the Acacias created an appealing campuslike setting for one of the nation's first continuing-care retirement communities.

When Dr. Andrus helped lay the cornerstone for the Acacias, in the spring of 1959, she was surrounded by people who represented all phases of her life and career. Participants in the ceremony included Alice Reiterman, her old basketball coach from Austin High in Chicago; Lincoln Andrus Service, M.D., Maud's eldest son, medical adviser for the Acacias project; and Ed Wenig, who had worked under Dr. Andrus as the drama teacher at Lincoln High (and whose former student Robert Preston was starring in *The Music Man,* the biggest hit on Broadway).

COMMUNITY SERVICE was an important element of Dr. Andrus' vision for instilling a sense of purpose in the members of NRTA and AARP. When Sumner Whittier, the head of the U.S. Veterans Administration, wanted to recruit members as potential volunteers, Dr. Andrus quickly embraced the offer.

She provided space in the *NRTA Journal* for a letter from Whittier that invited NRTA and AARP members to join the Veterans Administration Voluntary Service. This VA outreach program reflected Dr. Andrus' philosophy of "To serve, not to be served." It also advanced one of her

key goals: helping retirees recover the sense of purpose that many had lost when they gave up their jobs.

"You are needed!" That was the headline in the June 1959 *NRTA Journal* for an article urging members to volunteer at their local VA hospital.

"They will find their volunteer activities richly gratifying," Whittier wrote to Dr. Andrus, in his letter published alongside the journal article. "Your members can bring our patients something beyond the scope of medical science—a warmth and breadth of understanding that comes with having lived good, full years on this earth."

At the time, VA hospitals served many World War I veterans who were contemporaries of NRTA and AARP members. Many of these ailing former doughboys were lonely and depressed, as were some of Dr. Andrus' members, who faced social isolation after retiring. This was an opportunity to help themselves by helping others.

The VA program also generated considerable publicity for the newborn AARP, as Dr. Andrus noted in the August-September 1959 issue of *Modern Maturity*. Subsequent issues of the *NRTA Journal* and *Modern Maturity* carried dozens of articles and photos encouraging members to visit lonely veterans.

NEWSPAPERS COVERED THE NEW VA PROGRAM. →

V. A. HOSPITAL AID URGED

Volunteers Over 65 Sought to Give Service to Patients

Special to The New York Times.

WASHINGTON, June 12—A drive to enlist thousands of men and women 65 years old and older as volunteers in the 171 Veterans Administration Hospitals in the United States began today. It is being conducted by the Veterans Administration and the American

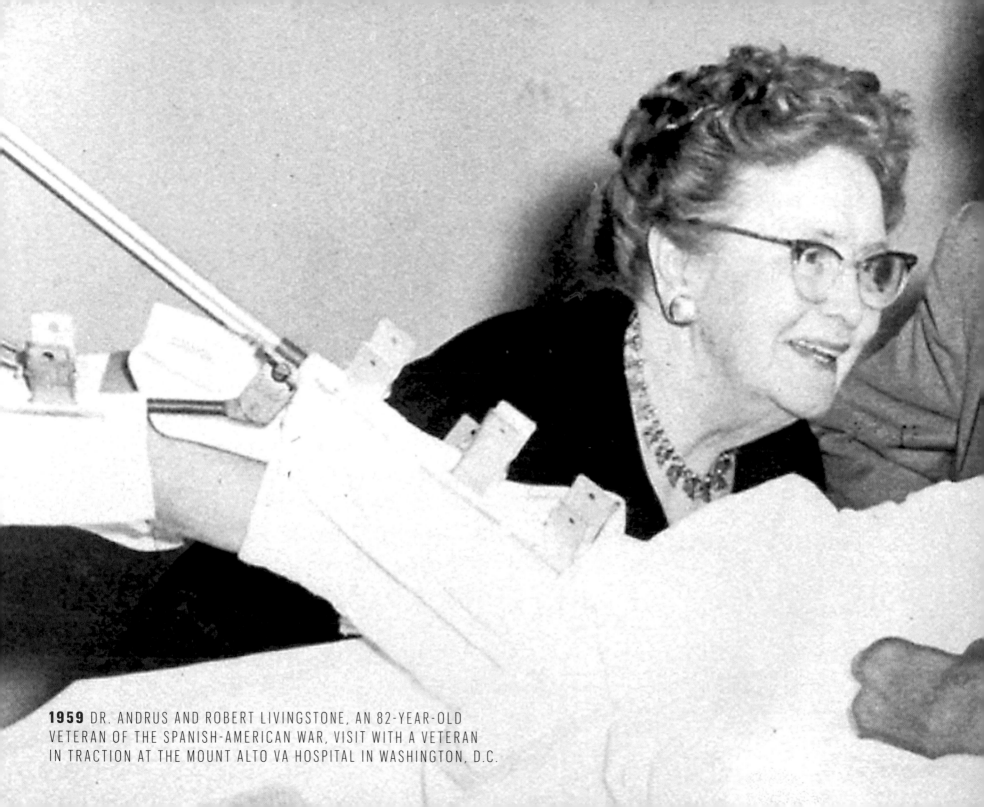

1959 DR. ANDRUS AND ROBERT LIVINGSTONE, AN 82-YEAR-OLD VETERAN OF THE SPANISH-AMERICAN WAR, VISIT WITH A VETERAN IN TRACTION AT THE MOUNT ALTO VA HOSPITAL IN WASHINGTON, D.C.

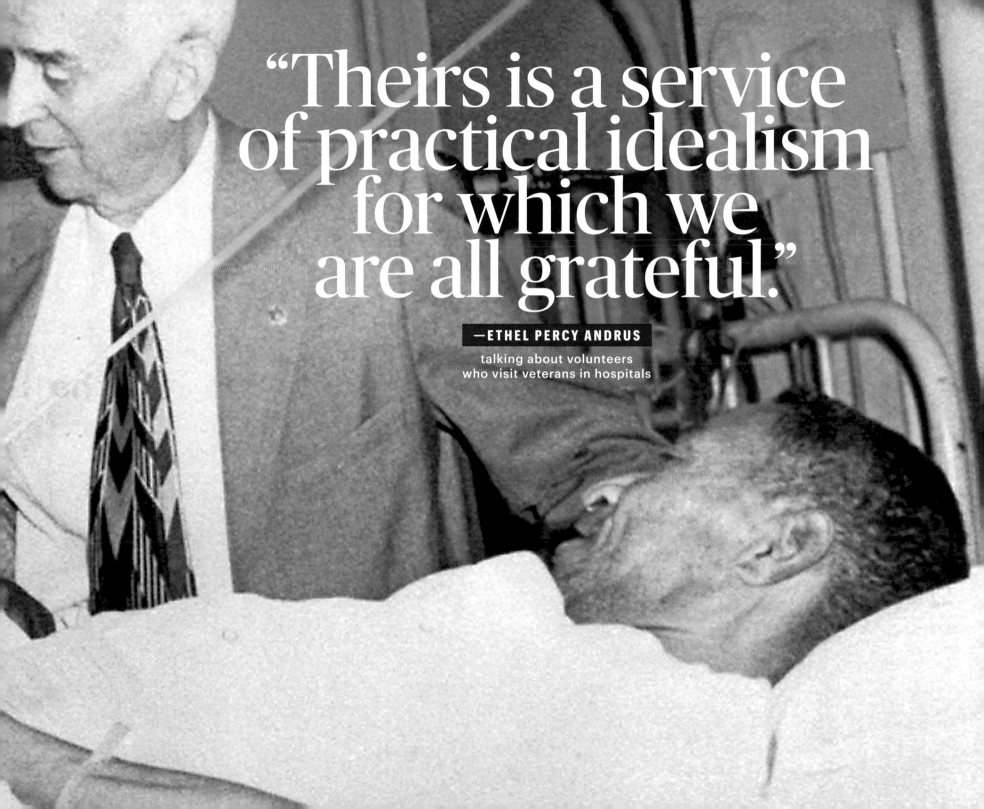

"Theirs is a service of practical idealism for which we are all grateful."

—ETHEL PERCY ANDRUS

talking about volunteers who visit veterans in hospitals

Drug Service Launches

WHEN READERS opened their June-July 1959 issue of *Modern Maturity,* they were confronted by a question: "Care to Increase Your Retirement Income?"

That was the headline over a questionnaire seeking input about a new market-changing pharmacy program. The idea was to leverage the group purchasing power of the 150,000 AARP and NRTA members to receive volume discounts from drug manufacturers. Long before warehouse and chain stores used bulk purchasing to save customers money, Dr. Andrus devised a plan to purchase medicines and vitamins in bulk and sell them to members, passing on the savings. AARP promised to make "nationally known standard brand medicines" available "at substantially reduced charges," with a startling new option: Drugs would be mailed directly to members' doors.

Members responded with predictable enthusiasm, and the first AARP pharmacy opened its door in Washington, D.C., in August 1959. A single registered pharmacist filled the prescriptions and delivered them to the post office

This 1959 survey helped AARP decide which medicines to offer and where to locate pharmacy outlets.

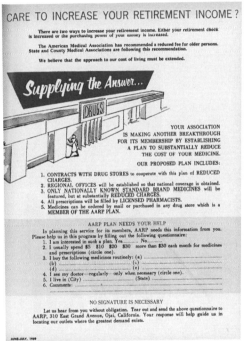

INNOVATIVE SERVICE
DR. ANDRUS (IN HAT) VISITS THE FIRST AARP-NRTA PHARMACY, LOCATED AT 4934 WISCONSIN AVE., NW, IN WASHINGTON, D.C.

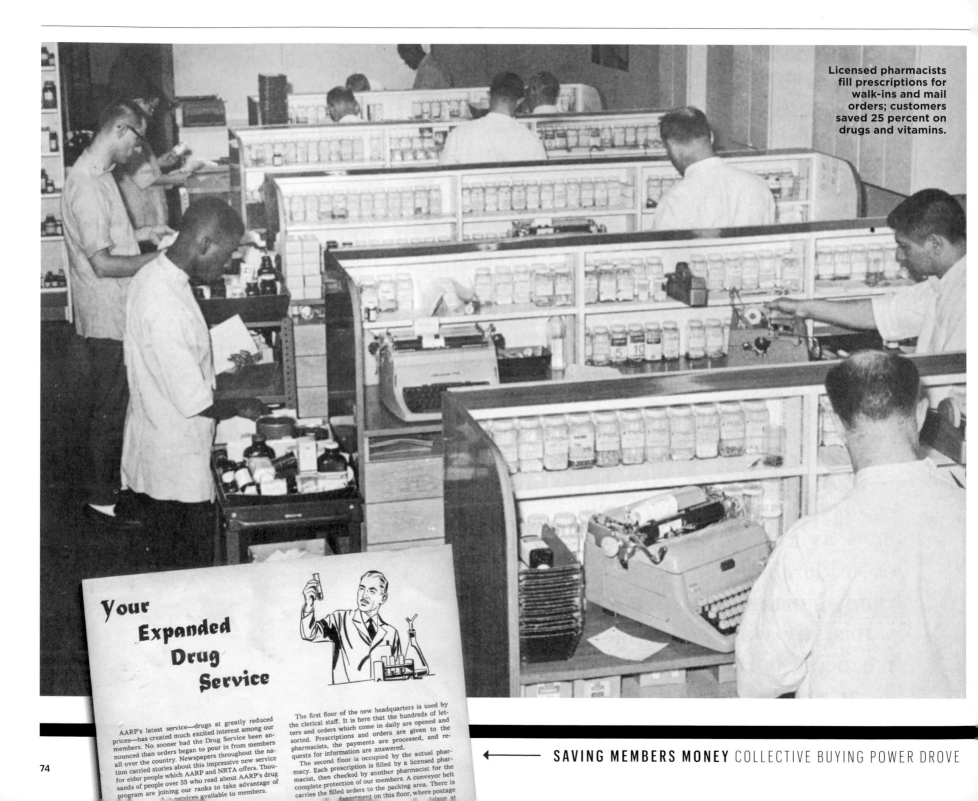

Licensed pharmacists fill prescriptions for walk-ins and mail orders; customers saved 25 percent on drugs and vitamins.

Your Expanded Drug Service

AARP's latest service—drugs at greatly reduced prices—has created much excited interest among our members. No sooner had the Drug Service been announced than orders began to pour in from members all over the country. Newspapers throughout the nation carried stories about this impressive new service for elder people which AARP and NRTA offers. Thousands of people over 55 who read about AARP's drug program are joining our ranks to take advantage of program are joining our ranks to take advantage of the services available to members.

The first floor of the new headquarters is used by the clerical staff. It is here that the hundreds of letters and orders which come in daily are opened and sorted. Prescriptions and orders are given to the pharmacists, the payments are processed, and requests for information are answered.

The second floor is occupied by the actual pharmacy. Each prescription is filled by a licensed pharmacist, then checked by another pharmacist for the complete protection of our members. A conveyor belt carries the filled orders to the packing area. There is a packing department on this floor, where postage

← **SAVING MEMBERS MONEY** COLLECTIVE BUYING POWER DROVE

himself on his way home. Members received discounts of at least 25 percent off retail list prices.

From this modest beginning, the nonprofit Drug Buying Service quickly expanded, arousing serious opposition from the pharmaceutical industry. Pharmaceuticals were the nation's most profitable industry, enjoying an average 22 percent profit margin, twice that of all manufacturers, according to a 1957 Federal Trade Commission study.

"We came so close to not being able to offer that mail-order drug service," recalled Bill Fitch, AARP's first executive director. "The pharmaceutical group was a real threat. You couldn't believe the kinds of things they were trying to do to embarrass AARP." Tactics included pushing federal legislation to make mail-order delivery of prescription drugs illegal and spreading untrue rumors that unlicensed people were filling prescriptions. Dr. Andrus responded to the industry's opposition: "Go ahead; it is about time the public knew the truth."

The battle soon moved to Congress. U.S. Senator Estes Kefauver of Tennessee—who made a name for himself in the early 1950s by investigating organized crime—was planning to investigate big drugmakers for alleged price gouging. One of the first witnesses before his Judiciary Committee subcommittee was Dr. Andrus, who named three drug manufacturers that refused to sell their medications to AARP's Washington pharmacy and that pressured the organization to close its first California pharmacy. Her testimony made the front page of the *New York Times* and other newspapers across the nation and led to the first of her several appearances on NBC's *Today* show.

The drug industry ended its efforts to snuff out AARP's discount pharmacy program, but rising prescription drug prices would continue to vex Dr. Andrus and AARP members for years.

Due in part to the visibility Dr. Andrus had achieved through her legislative victory on retired teachers' federal taxes, pioneering marketplace innovations and promotion of a new image of aging, she was appointed, in June 1959, to the national advisory committee charged

Dr. Andrus and Ruth Lana, executive director of NRTA-AARP services, at the Long Beach pharmacy

"You speak for people who need to be spoken for."

–U.S. Senator Estes Kefauver, at a 1961 hearing on drug industry prices and practices, speaking about Dr. Andrus' advocacy

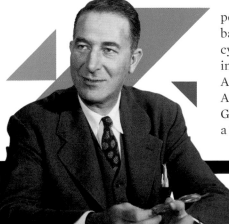

with preparing the White House Conference on Aging, scheduled to convene in January 1961.

Aging had made its way to the national agenda. "Few advisory committees have received a more significant assignment," Health, Education and Welfare Secretary Arthur S. Flemming told its members. "There are almost 50 million Americans who are 45 years of age and older in our country today whose economic security, employment and retirement problems—including health and medical care, recreation, housing, and social and civic participation—will be a major concern of the White House Conference on Aging."

The nation's capital was becoming increasingly important for AARP. Executive Director Bill Fitch was based there, as were Ruth Lana, running the travel agency, and Grace Hatfield, still administering the group insurance plans. Dr. Andrus was frequently there, too. AARP's national headquarters remained in Ojai, and Dr. Andrus continued to maintain her official residence in Grey Gables, but for all practical purposes she was now a Washingtonian.

CHAPTER 6

"NOT TO BE FORGO OR

Dr. Andrus introduced an innovative universal design home, aptly named the House of Freedom.

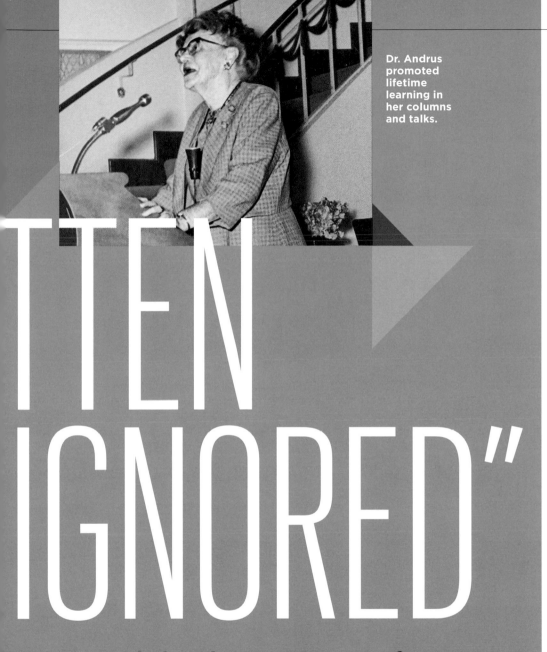

Dr. Andrus promoted lifetime learning in her columns and talks.

TTEN IGNORED"

Bold champion for older Americans

NSCONCED NOW IN the national scene, Dr. Ethel Percy Andrus traveled to Chicago in July 1960 to address the Republican Party, which was nominating Richard Nixon for president. She was there to educate the party's Platform Committee on four essential needs of all Americans: decent living conditions, good health, adequate housing and meaning in life. (Bill Fitch, the executive director of NRTA and AARP, had already presented a similar statement in Los Angeles to the Platform Committee of the Democratic Party, which had nominated John F. Kennedy.)

Dr. Andrus cast in stark terms the challenge facing Republicans in drafting their platform on human needs: economic hardships facing older adults and younger individuals feeling more secure, thanks to Social Security and work-based retirement savings. Dr. Andrus told the GOP Platform Committee: "You are dealing with two segments of the aging group: first, those of the aged-aged who engineered America through a Depression and two world wars, who earned their salaries in a different economic world, with wages low-geared, meeting the sudden shock of mandatory retirement, with insurance rare and denied the elderly, with little earned or no Social Security benefits, with the Depression and inflation eating away their savings and their property, their only guilt being that they have lived too long."

This "aged-aged" group, Dr. Andrus went on, "denied the right to work, now often disabled and infirm, poorly housed and fearful of the future, with small income increasingly growing smaller in purchasing power by forces beyond their control, have problems which now become your problems."

The second group is younger, she said, "nearly always protected by Social Security and often safeguarded by company-paid retirement programs and insurance."

She urged party members to adopt policies (at right) to help both groups live independently and with dignity.

Although she normally felt passionate about limiting government involvement in citizens' lives, Dr. Andrus recognized that private-sector organizations like NRTA and AARP could not solve these profound problems on their own.

"Volunteer groups cannot hope to meet the needs of the impoverished aging," she told the panel. "This is and must be the concern of government."

Dr. Andrus also summarized NRTA and AARP's accomplishments, including the health plans and the discount pharmacy, established despite the initial indifference of the insurance industry and opposition from major drug companies.

"The recital of our achievements sounds like boasting," she said. "Perhaps so, but I am telling you this story of our volunteer efforts done in a truly American manner, impelled by our faith in the freedom of choice and the responsibility of self-help."

Dr. Andrus' vigor reflected her passion for civic engagement and a commitment to tackling pressing issues facing people as they aged. The politicians she addressed on that sweltering Chicago day in 1960 saw a demurely dressed, highly respectable, soft-spoken 78-year-old woman—who put them on notice that retirees now constituted a large and powerful constituency and that AARP would serve as its voice.

And also as its ear. The 1960 presidential election inaugurated *Modern Maturity*'s practice of soliciting the positions of both presidential nominees regarding issues affecting older Americans.

The organization's message was coming through loud and clear: Older Americans had needs, they had rights, and they could harness their lifetime of experience to make positive changes for people of all ages.

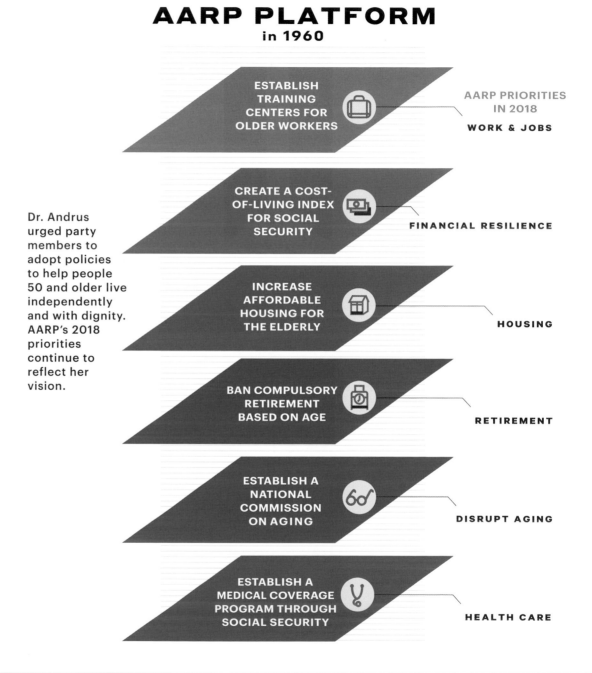

Dr. Andrus urged party members to adopt policies to help people 50 and older live independently and with dignity. AARP's 2018 priorities continue to reflect her vision.

AARP PLATFORM
in 1960

	AARP PRIORITIES IN 2018
ESTABLISH TRAINING CENTERS FOR OLDER WORKERS	WORK & JOBS
CREATE A COST-OF-LIVING INDEX FOR SOCIAL SECURITY	FINANCIAL RESILIENCE
INCREASE AFFORDABLE HOUSING FOR THE ELDERLY	HOUSING
BAN COMPULSORY RETIREMENT BASED ON AGE	RETIREMENT
ESTABLISH A NATIONAL COMMISSION ON AGING	DISRUPT AGING
ESTABLISH A MEDICAL COVERAGE PROGRAM THROUGH SOCIAL SECURITY	HEALTH CARE

THE LITTLE WHITE HOUSE CONFERENCE ON AGING

The nonpartisan recommendations that Dr. Andrus and Bill Fitch presented to the political parties in the summer of 1960 reflected input from a cross section of older Americans at an NRTA-AARP conference at the Coliseum (above) in St. Petersburg, Florida, in January 1960. That gathering's purpose was to help develop programs to improve life for older people, as a prelude to the 1961 White House Conference on Aging. "Here 1,500 older persons discussed ... the problems of aging from the aged person's viewpoint and made their recommendations," Dr. Andrus said of the Florida meeting, dubbed the Little White House Conference. These suggestions reflected AARP's goals for retirees: decent living conditions, good health, adequate housing and meaning in life.

AARP'S FIRST LOCAL CHAPTERS

1. Youngtown, Arizona
2. Wayne, West Virginia
3. Hot Springs National Park, Arkansas
4. Sun City, Arizona
5. Kansas City, Missouri
6. St. Joseph, Missouri
7. Pontiac, Michigan
8. Hendersonville, North Carolina
9. Port City of Muskegon County, Michigan
10. San Gorgonio Pass, California

Busting Isolation

WHILE DRAWING MEMBERS' attention to national politics, Dr. Andrus also built strong communities of AARP members at the local level.

In September 1960, AARP chartered its first local chapter, in Youngtown, Arizona. Chapters provided opportunities for members to discuss common interests, volunteer together for community service projects and collaborate with other local groups to study community problems affecting older people. Following Youngtown, chapters began springing up across the country, allowing AARP members to connect more effectively with one another. District offices operated on the regional level, channeling feedback and ideas to Dr. Andrus and her colleagues.

Most important, chapters sparked new friendships.

"The AARP brotherhood is magic medicine for the lonely," Dr. Andrus wrote in a *Modern Maturity* column. "I often wonder if we who have a rich home life realize the cruel and crippling sense of loneliness that seems to rob its victim of a compelling purpose for life and even the sense of personal identity.

"I believe that we cannot stress too strongly this problem that older people, on losing their dear ones, often face stark loneliness in our restless urban America. I have seen men and women housed in these pigeon crofts that we city folk call apartments find in the meeting of other AARP folk a fortunate relief."

New Ways of Living

HOUSING, in Dr. Andrus' view, was critical to connecting people to community life. She was seeing it firsthand in Ojai, at Grey Gables. This experiment in designed communal living for retirees was now six years old, and Dr. Andrus was determined to build on its success. She had conceived it as a pilot program; it was time to apply the lessons learned at Grey Gables and at the Acacias health center next door to meet the housing needs of retired people across the country, whether they lived communally or in their own homes. *Modern Maturity* in April-May 1960 detailed AARP's plans:

"There is a growing awareness of the need for housing for the elderly and a widespread desire, on the part of many groups, to do something about [it]. This mounting interest reveals a need AARP is eager to serve. ... It is studying techniques, planning for various types of facilities, and exploring the problems of financing. Its pur-

HOUSING PLANS IN
MODERN MATURITY
↓

pose is to offer to its membership, without fee, a series of workable plans for the financing and construction of retirement homes. AARP is now busily engaged in the time-consuming and expensive research preparatory to this new service. We believe that its findings and recommendations will do much to facilitate the founding of such homes throughout the nation."

Group living, of course, was the housing option chosen by Dr. Andrus herself, at Grey Gables, and *Modern Maturity* explored it in considerable detail. An article in the October-November 1960 issue trumpeted "the pleasures of living in a retirement village" by focusing on places such as Youngtown, Arizona, the home of AARP's first local chapter and first community to restrict its residents to people over a certain age.

Dr. Andrus continued to use *Modern Maturity* to share new research on retirement living to help her readers envision new ways to live.

"The first requisite for good housing, of any type, is the assurance of maximum quiet, independence and privacy, yet so located and designed as to permit the residents to keep in touch with neighbors, with life and activity in the community," Whitney R. Smith, an award-winning architect, wrote in a seven-page article for the August-September 1960 issue.

Retirees who remained in their homes should consider remodeling them, Smith wrote, to eliminate steep stairs and high cupboards and other elements that would soon become standard universal design features.

Wherever retirees decided to live, what they needed from a home, according to Smith, was "convenience, satisfaction and dignity, and at a reasonable price."

To show the possibilities of retiree-friendly architecture, Dr. Andrus commissioned a universal design home in St. Petersburg, the first of what she called a House of Freedom, and then prepared another version for the White House Conference on Aging.

HOUSING for the elderly

Elevation of one end of a twin unit..

Whitney R. Smith, Chairman
by Retirement Home Planners*

Low cost housing for the elderly is becoming an ever increasing need. Meeting this need adequately

GARDEN APARTMENTS Retirees planning to buy new homes might consider compact homes, which would be less expensive and easier to maintain and navigate.

TRAILER PARKS Trailers provided compact and affordable housing. They sometimes came furnished, and they were set in small communities to increase social ties.

RETIREMENT COMMUNITIES A newer Arizona retiree community, Sun City, offered a good model. It featured a nine-hole golf course, a ceramics studio complete with kiln, and transportation to shops.

REMODELING People who wanted to stay in their homes were encouraged to add universal design features such as wide entrances and, in bathrooms, grab bars and nonslip tile floors.

Conference on Aging

ON JANUARY 9, 1961, Dr. Andrus was in Constitution Hall in Washington, D.C., as outgoing President Dwight D. Eisenhower opened the first White House Conference on Aging—a conference that continues today. "This is the last time I shall have the privilege of bidding welcome to a group of Americans assembled here in the capital city to confer among themselves about problems interesting to a particular group or indeed to the whole nation," said President Eisenhower, then 70 and the oldest person ever to hold the office. "This one, of course, is about the problems of the aged or the aging, because I don't want to get too definite about this aged business!"

Two days later, Dr. Andrus visited the White House and presented President Eisenhower with the keys to a universal design home built with AARP's support (see page 84), along with a scale model for him to inspect. Her column for the next issue of *Modern Maturity* pronounced the White House Conference on Aging "a great success!"

"The concept of the conference recognized that the development of a wholesome climate for 'aging with a future' is the concern and responsibility of everyone in our land," she wrote. "For far too many people, aging has

During the first White House Conference on Aging, Dr. Andrus presented to President Eisenhower a model of AARP's universal design house.

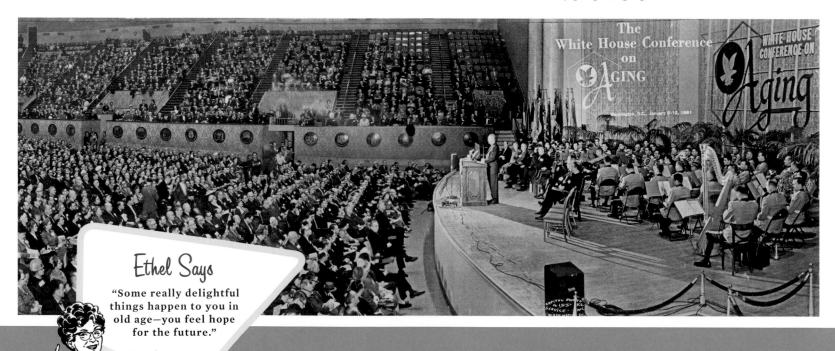

Ethel Says

"Some really delightful things happen to you in old age—you feel hope for the future."

meant inadequate income, poor or marginal health, isolation, unacceptable housing and the bitterness of being shunted aside from the mainstream of life."

She noted with satisfaction that the Conference on Aging had recommended several ideas that she had been advocating, including eliminating compulsory retirement and developing a Senior Citizens' Charter of Rights, which included the following tenets:

1 The right to be useful
2 The right to attain employment based on merit
3 The right to freedom from want in old age
4 The right to a full share of community, recreational, educational and medical resources
5 The right to obtain decent housing suited to needs of later years
6 The right to moral and financial support by one's family, as far as is consistent with the best interests of the family
7 The right to live independently
8 The right to live, to die, with dignity
9 The right of access to all knowledge as available on how to improve the later years of life

A MONTH AFTER President-elect Kennedy addressed the closing session of the White House Conference on Aging, Dr. Andrus' sister, Maud Andrus Service, died, at the age of 82.

For Ethel Percy Andrus, this was another watershed moment. Maud was her elder sister, whom she had grown up admiring personally and professionally. Maud had been the first of the two to become a teacher, and she had worked with her sister for two decades at Lincoln High School. And Maud had been a fellow Grey Gables pioneer and, later, had helped Dr. Andrus create *Modern Maturity* and served as one of AARP's founding directors.

House of Freedom

Washington, D.C.

AFTER HELPING RETIREES imagine how to live affordably yet in style, Dr. Andrus helped pull off a new innovation: a universal design home for older people. The compact House of Freedom, in downtown Washington, D.C., was toured by an estimated 3,000 attendees of the 1961 White House Conference on Aging.

The builder said he called it the House of Freedom because it provided "freedom from household drudgery, from poor lighting, from dangerously slick floors or stairways, from expensive housing expense."

NRTA and AARP cosponsored the home, which was built by the Douglas Fir Plywood Association (now APA–The Engineered Wood Association). Careful research into active adults' needs yielded features that, sadly, are still not widely available today: no-step entries, nonskid floors, wide doorways and, in the bathroom, grab bars.

Dr. Andrus and executives of the Douglas Fir Plywood Association presented the key to the House of Freedom to President Eisenhower at the White House.

← THE HOUSE OF FREEDOM'S MODERN INTERIOR

JANUARY 1961
COST $9,000

WHAT MADE IT SPECIAL?

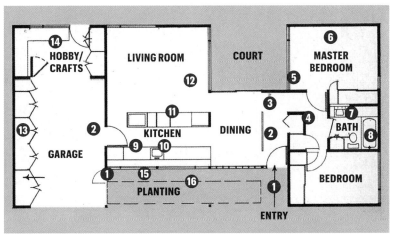

Floor plan labels: HOBBY/CRAFTS, LIVING ROOM, COURT, MASTER BEDROOM, KITCHEN, DINING, BATH, GARAGE, BEDROOM, PLANTING, ENTRY

1 No-step entries for safer access

2 Master light switches at both entrances

3 Nonskid floors throughout the home

4 Doors and hallways at least 3 feet wide for walkers and wheelchairs

5 Electrical outlets 18 inches above floors, making them easier to access

6 Master light switch in master bedroom

7 Dressing seat next to bathtub

8 Grab bars in bathroom to prevent falls

9 Lower cabinets in kitchen raised off the floor; upper cabinets at height within easy reach

10 Low sink for sit-down dishwashing

11 Pull-down light fixtures for easier bulb replacement

12 Perimeter heat throughout the home for warm floors

13 Extra storage space in garage

14 Hobby/crafts area in garage

15 Outdoor water faucets at least 24 Inches above ground

16 Wide roof overhang surrounding the home to protect people from rain

Hospitality House

St. Petersburg, Florida

A **NDRUS' CHOICE** of St. Petersburg, "the Sunshine City," as the site for both her Little White House Conference and for Hospitality House was not a coincidence. Florida was now a major haven for older Americans, whether they were retirees moving permanently to the Sunshine State or snowbirds from northern states seeking a winter respite from the cold weather.

Hospitality House offered a place for retirees to gather and make new friends at its afternoon social hours and to find information about sightseeing and other activities. In some ways, it was a forerunner of today's senior centers.

"As surely as the fall is beautiful and colorful, the winter comes stark and cold," *Modern Maturity* noted in a typical article touting Hospitality House. "Why break your back and stop your heart shoveling snow when you can bask in the warmth of the 'Sunshine City?'

"You'll have loads of fun in St. Petersburg," *Modern Maturity* assured its readers. "So pack up your swim suits and sweaters, neckties and sports shirts, suits and evening dresses and be prepared to have a big time making these latter years your best years."

AARP would open a second Hospitality House, in Long Beach, California, in 1962, and a third, in Washington, D.C., in 1963. All three had AARP discount pharmacies nearby. The Florida location operated its own hotel.

You'll find warm hospitality in St. Petersburg

Margaret H. Stine, Director

Hospitality Houses helped members strike up friendships, be creative and stay active and engaged.

> "Don't just retire *from* something— retire *to* something. We will help you to recreate."
>
> –Margaret Stine, director, St. Petersburg Hospitality House

CHAPTER 7

"DYNAMIC MATUR

The Institute of Lifelong Learning tied directly into Dr. Andrus' philosophy of dynamic maturity.

The New York World's Fair, where NRTA-AARP had a contemporary exhibit

ITY"

The future is our business

EMPOWERED BY a combined NRTA and AARP membership now exceeding 500,000, and inspired by the 1961 White House Conference on Aging, Dr. Ethel Percy Andrus became even more vigorous in serving as a nonpartisan spokesperson for older Americans' needs.

She was already a familiar presence in Washington, D.C., having testified on such topics as mandatory retirement and housing for senior citizens. Now Dr. Andrus threw the organizations' growing influence behind Senator Estes Kefauver's bill to increase federal regulation of the pharmaceutical industry—an industry that she had come to know in launching the NRTA-AARP nonprofit prescription drug service.

Most of her members lived on fixed incomes, she testified, so they could not keep up with the rising prices of prescription drugs. "Their ability to purchase the needed drugs often makes the difference between sickness and health and sometimes between life and death," she said.

Dr. Andrus hit the industry's monopolistic practices head-on. "Your hearings have shown that a few large drug companies have a complete monopoly over the production of certain leading ethical drugs," she testified. "The question is not how this came about. The question is why it should continue.

"The facts are that a few large companies do retain this rigid control, and we believe the people of the country, through their committees and the Congress, will take necessary and proper measures to assure that the medical discoveries for the treatment of sickness are made available to more of our people at a price they can afford."

Although she believed in limited government, Dr. Andrus noted that "a government of the people is occasionally compelled by the cries of distressed citizens to come to their protection through legislative means."

Over tremendous opposition from the drug industry, Kefauver's landmark bill became law in 1962. Known as the Kefauver-Harris Amendments, it controlled the marketing of generic drugs to keep prices down and established a framework that required drug manufacturers to prove scientifically that a medication was safe and effective. The new law also gave the U.S. Food and Drug Administration more power to combat medical quackery, an effort Dr. Andrus strongly backed. Fraud, she had found, was an increasing concern among her members.

The next year, she was invited to be the lead witness in a U.S. Senate hearing about frauds affecting the elderly. "Charlatans," she testified, often exploited older persons who were too proud or embarrassed to report their victimization. For her part, she pledged to undertake a major educational program to empower members to prevent fraud.

And so, as the FDA began using its new authority to take medical charlatans to court, Dr. Andrus used the pages of *Modern Maturity* and NRTA-AARP conventions to alert members that Americans were being swindled out of at least $1 billion a year on falsely promoted, worthless or dangerous products and treatments.

OPERATION PHILANTHROPY is how Dr. Andrus described one of NRTA and AARP's most far-reaching activities to date: the Retirement Research and Welfare Association, created in 1961 as part of her "crusade for the welfare of the individual." This third affiliate was, Dr. Andrus said, an "organization of persons interested in the field of aging, studying retirement living as experienced by older persons where needed, and seeking to find solutions to better such conditions."

Members' donations to the nonprofit helped combat "medical quackery," gather and tabulate more than 11,000 responses to a questionnaire on employment after retirement and assist the Library of Congress in provid-

Dr. Andrus (left) and Dorothy Crippen present a $1,000 check to Librarian of Congress L. Quincy Mumford in 1963 to record books for the blind.

ing audio recordings of books so that people with sight impairments could continue reading and learning.

Dr. Andrus appointed Dorothy Crippen, her cousin and treasured colleague, as director of the Retirement Research and Welfare Association. The Internal Revenue Service granted it tax-exempt status in 1963, further promoting its charitable and philanthropic activities.

A fourth affiliate, the Association of Retired Persons International, was created in 1963, when Dr. Andrus realized that more than 1,000 members resided outside the United States. ARP International was "a nongovernmental and nonpolitical organization with the aims and functions of dignifying and refining retirement living among older people the world over and to challenge older persons to grow and to serve."

The AARP-supported International Federation on Aging replaced ARP International in 1973, but ARP International's motto—"To serve, not to be served" (written on its seal in Latin as *administrare non administrari*—remains AARP's motto today, a hallmark of its social mission, which includes ongoing global outreach.

ANDRUS ENJOYED spectacular success with another early 1960s initiative: an NRTA-AARP exhibit at the New York World's Fair.

New York City was planning a two-year world's fair to open in April 1964, and tens of millions of people were expected to attend. "Peace through understanding" was the theme, but the main idea was to dazzle fairgoers with futuristic exhibits showcasing space-age technology and midcentury-modern architecture. The biggest corporations in the United States were spending lavishly to create eye-catching pavilions, many of which featured that newfangled invention, the computer.

For the planners, Dr. Andrus had a pertinent question: Would any of the expected exhibits focus specifically on older people? The answer was, unsurprisingly, no. Nonprofit advocacy groups were welcome to participate as exhibitors, but few could afford to do so. AARP was an exception, and Dr. Andrus seized the opportunity to bring her message to that potentially enormous audience.

"Never has AARP felt more proud than on Aug. 13, 1962, when, on the same day, it was invited ... as the outstanding organization for older people in the nation by the New York World's Fair Executive Committee and by seven different branches of the U.S. government interested in various phases of aging and retirement," she wrote in AARP's *News Bulletin*.

"We were convinced that the resurgence of faith in the potentialities of maturity was a great social revolution of much importance," she later recalled. "And so the deci-

World, Meet AARP

← **WORLD'S FAIR** THE NRTA-AARP DYNAMIC MATURITY PAVILION SHOWCASED A NEW IMAGE OF AGING.

"Independence of spirit, pride in continued performance, dignity and self-respect ... are not exclusive properties of the young."

—ETHEL PERCY ANDRUS

talking about the Dynamic Maturity Pavilion

sion was reached that the dynamic change of attitude toward age ... must be featured in the World's Fair."

The pavilion's title, Dynamic Maturity, said it all. The timing was perfect. The United States in the 1960s was being swept up in the youth culture of post World War II. Young baby boomers were expected to visit the fair in droves. Dr. Andrus proudly noted that for the first time in the history of world's fairs, visitors would be exposed to the idea that older people still had contributions to make to society.

The Dynamic Maturity entrance was dominated by a massive sundial—20 feet in diameter, designed by sculptor Herbert Feuerlicht—in keeping with the concept of time being ageless. Visitors with physical limitations could tour the pavilion with ease, since its design reflected the American Standards Association's accessibility guidelines, which had been distributed by fair planners.

Inside, most of the exhibit space highlighted NRTA-AARP and their programs to help retirees lead fuller, healthier lives. But one of the exhibit's most popular features was a camera obscura, which used mirrors to reflect images of the surrounding areas onto a large round floor in the middle of the building.

"Dr. Andrus wanted the exhibit to be something that was educational, something distinctive," recalled Bill Fitch, executive director of NRTA and AARP. "She said that one of the most exciting things she could remember as a girl was a camera obscura."

She had seen it at Woodward's Gardens, an amusement park near the Andrus family home in San Francisco. Although that park was long gone by 1963, the exhibit designers located an old camera obscura that could serve as a model for the Dynamic Maturity version.

Nearby exhibitors at the fair included such corporate heavyweights as Coca-Cola and DuPont, which spared no expense to create first-class pavilions. Yet Dynamic Maturity looked contemporary and drew impressive crowds, indicating that NRTA-AARP could be as distinctive and innovative as the larger sponsors.

In a way, this fair brought Dr. Andrus full circle. The

NRTA-AARP EXHIBIT

1 Kurt Ard Gallery
2 Reception area
3 Camera obscura
4 Hall of Fame
5 Exhibit of nine U.S. areas
6 NRTA-AARP Service showcase
7 Conference area
8 Garden of Achievement
9 Camera Pavilion

Chicago World's Fair of her youth had presented an inspiring vision of America's future, which more or less had arrived in due course. Now the New York World's Fair presented a new vision of the future, and Dr. Andrus wanted retirees to be part of it.

"The AARP with its own exhibit at the World's Fair in New York made a very significant statement," Fitch said. "There were no other senior organizations represented there. We had an attractive, not inexpensive exhibit. ... It sent a message not only to people of this country but around the world."

In addition to acquainting hundreds of thousands of visitors with NRTA and AARP, Dr. Andrus used the Dynamic Maturity Pavilion to hold one-day meetings with business leaders and religious groups to discuss their needs and long-range plans.

At the first meeting, 13 corporate executives talked about "What American Industry Is Doing to Prepare Their

Employees for Retirement" with Bill Fitch. Participants hailed from Bostich, Coca-Cola, General Foods, the National Association of Manufacturers and other heavy hitters, who shared best practices—as well as frustrations—for preretirement planning and for tapping the skills of recently retired workers.

One participant commented, "I hoped today to learn many things of how to form a plan or program—education, monetary problems, fears; medical fears are a big factor here." Another quipped that the wives of recent retirees were frustrated about the new arrangement: "Twice as much husband and half as much income."

At the second meeting, the following June, diverse members of the United Church Women of the National Council of Churches gathered. Subsequent meetings were held around the country with representatives of other faith-based groups. Fitch later said, "There is widespread concern and sincere interest on the part of religious leaders that more information, guidance and counseling should be given through the churches and synagogues to their older members."

At the fair (clockwise from top left): NRTA-AARP legislative agenda; Ruth Lana, Dr. Andrus and Dorothy Crippen alight from a Greyhound Escorter; Dr. Andrus in front of the display for the camera obscura with Dorothy Crippen; Crippen, Lana, Dr. Andrus' nephew Lincoln Service and a visitor look at a model of Grey Gables; the meeting of the United Church Women of the National Council of Churches.

Learning Is Timeless

President John F. Kennedy welcomes older Peace Corps volunteers. Dr. Andrus was an early and vocal proponent of the program.

ODERN MATURITY and the *NRTA Journal* publicized the world's fair, urging readers to attend. Still, AARP's publications—and Dr. Andrus herself—also remained firmly focused on activities in Washington, D.C., where legislators were addressing the recommendations of the White House Conference on Aging.

The new president, John F. Kennedy, had created the President's Council on Aging by executive order. But making real progress on these issues would require congressional action. In February 1963, Kennedy sent Congress a message that read as though Dr. Andrus herself had written it:

"The heart of our program for the elderly must be opportunity for and actual service to our older citizens in their home communities. The loneliness or apathy which exists among many of our aged is heightened by the wall of inertia which often exists between them and their community. We must remove this wall by planned, comprehensive action to stimulate or provide not only opportunities for employment and community services by our older citizens but the full range of the various facilities and services which aged individuals need for comfortable and meaningful life. ... The federal government can assume a significant leadership role in stimulating such action."

Congressman John E. Fogarty of Rhode Island, whose bill had created the White House Conference on Aging, began crafting legislation to incorporate Kennedy's recommendations. Fogarty eventually introduced it as the Older Americans Act, noting it was supported by expert testimony from leaders of AARP, NRTA and the Association of Retired Persons International, which together represented "a paid membership of more than 700,000 individuals."

Although the Older Americans Act wasn't passed the first year it was introduced, momentum was building for Congress to address the issues, and Dr. Andrus was prominent among its advocates.

MEANWHILE, Dr. Andrus' philosophy that "life is a journey, not a destination" sparked the founding of an educational program for dynamic maturity, the Institute of Lifetime Learning, which opened at AARP's Washington headquarters in September 1963.

The *Washington Post* took notice. Students at the institute, the newspaper reported, "will 'reeducate' themselves in everything from typing to international affairs, from gift-making to art, from politics and government to taking the old-lady-look out of old clothes." New classes are presented each session, and plans are always being made for additional courses of appeal to the students. "Cost per class will be less than the price of a movie. ... Outlook for the future? Horizons unlimited."

"We are changing the image of elderly persons from shuffleboard to academic studies."

–Joe Gunn, dean of the NRTA-AARP Institute of Lifetime Learning

Nineteen years had passed since Dr. Andrus had retired as the Lincoln High School principal, but she remained an educator at heart. The night school for adults she had established at Lincoln High was still thriving. And she had watched with interest as her alma mater, the University of Chicago, expanded its University College, an adult education division.

"A considerable amount of continuing learning is essential to a satisfying, productive life," Dr. Andrus wrote in the *NRTA Journal* in 1952, in an article describing the Chicago Lifetime Learning program. "A deeper understanding of our society, a fuller appreciation of the moral and aesthetic values of our civilization, a greater ability to participate in the democratic process of self-government—these are the areas in which the maturing individual discovers his educational needs."

Off to an enthusiastic start – The Institute of Lifetime Learning

Flower arranging is a consuming art of working with form, texture and color.

Shorthand is a challenge to an alert mind and nimble

The thought that *life is a journey, not a destination* sparked the founding of the Institute of Lifetime Learning. And the overwhelming response to the truth of the program in Washington has testified to the truth of the Institute's motto: Age is timeless. The eagerness to learn — to pioneer in the development of new skills and new abilities, to broaden the personal scopes of understanding, to freshen the mind with new ideas and new concepts — knows no limitations in the restrictions of time. For intellectual curiosity generates and sustains a youthful vigor and enthusiasm that defies age in its continuous manifestation of hardy, new growth. And to grow — to create new life in the form of new thoughts and ideas from an existing storehouse of knowledge and experience — is an extending of the vitality for a life of dignity and independence through usefulness.

Fortified with the encouraging acceptance of this, our first of ten-week sessions, it is hoped that the Institute of Lifetime Learning will also conduct vigorous new growth. As it expands to serve ever-

expanding areas of the country, it is also hoped that it will grow to widen its scope — to better serve by encompassing more areas of interest for even greater challenges and opportunities.

In its youthful beginning, classes are now offered in arts, crafts, secretarial, speech, photography, English, music appreciation, international relations, government in action and preparation for dynamic maturity.

The Institute's student body vibrates with a multiplicity of ambitions in search of new knowledge. All are explorers — are fired with a zeal to seek out new careers of interest. Some are preparing for part-new careers of interest. Others are seeking to fill in gaps of new employment. Still others are impelled to fulfill lifelong desires to ready themselves for community leadership. The atmosphere of the classrooms is electrified with the single joy of doing, the ringing thrill of accomplishment and the satisfying rewards that come from the courage to try.

MODERN MATURITY

Through the Institute's vast panorama of related activities the American Association of Retired Persons is enjoying a great and exhilarating experience in service. In this short formative period of gratifying response has come from the four corners of America. More and more communities asking how they can establish a local Institute of Lifetime Learning . . . they like the "Every Wednesday Morning series; they like the idea of regular classroom activity; they like the thought of opening new doors of opportunity to the mature citizens in their particular communities.

To all of the interested communities throughout the country we shall be grateful for an opportunity to work with them and delighted to offer every possible assistance. The Institute of Lifetime Learning is, in essence, another expression of the Association's belief that age is timeless — that boundless energy can achieve new heights of knowledge in continuous growth has no age restrictions.

DECEMBER-JANUARY 1963-64

58

THE WORLD'S GREAT RELIGIONS

Mohammedanism or Islam

Islam is based on the belief in one God called Allah. The main tenet of this faith is, "There is no god but Allah, and Mohammed is his prophet."

This religion dates back to the story of Abraham and Ishmael whom the Arabian people revered as their forefathers. The story tells that a chieftain named Abraham banished to the desert his son Ishmael and his wife, Hagar.

Hagar feared they would die of thirst, but young Ishmael kicked the hot sand and a spring of water gushed forth. When Abraham heard of the miracle, he named the spring Zamzam, and nearby he built a temple called Kaaba. In it he set the Black Stone which reputedly had come to him as an inheritance from Adam from the Garden of Eden, when Adam and Eve were banished.

Near their temple Hagar and her son continued to live at the site which became known as Mecca. Ishmael grew up and married, and

as was told in the Koran and likewise in the Old Testament, the children of Ishmael took possession of the land, which became a great nation. Mecca became the sacred city of these people to which they made pilgrimages to worship in the temple, to kiss the Black Stone, and to drink of the sacred waters of Zamzam.

Mecca also became the prosperous transfer city on the ancient route between India and Syria. As it grew, perfidious customs became intermingled with the religious ceremonies.

In 570 A.D. Mohammed was born in Mecca into an aristocratic family of the Koreish tribe. Legends arose later about the many miracles that accompanied his birth and how omens foretold that he would cleanse the earth of idolatry and corruption.

His father died shortly before he was born and his mother when he was six. Mohammed was left to the care of his grandfather, a camel

driver, who took the boy with him on long caravan journeys into far countries. Here, Mohammed heard of the beliefs of Judaism and Christianity and acquired a growing respect for belief in one powerful God. On these long, monotonous desert crossings he meditated on the history of his own people and how they could be won away from idolatry and the evil practices which had debated them.

One day he stated that he heard a "voice" commanding him, "Oh, Mohammed, you are Allah's messenger and I am Gabriel." Revelations, reputedly, continued to come to him, and the visions commanded him to preach.

At first people scoffed, but a faithful few gave him courage and he continued to tell of his visions and spoke against corruption and against idols. His opponents finally plotted to kill him and he was forced to flee. The night of his flight, *hegira*, June 20, 622 A.D., has become a most memorable date, known as Year One of the founding of the Mohammedan religion.

He fled to Medina where he or-

ganized an army, and gained many converts to his new faith, which he called *Islam*, meaning "Submission to the one and only God of Allah." This "new" faith he proclaimed as the true religion of their forefathers, Abraham and Ishmael.

History gives another version, that it was the modification of the faith of a small group of thoughtful persons called *Hanifs* or "penitents" and that this faith of the Hanifs was strongly influenced by the early faiths of the Jews, Christians, the followers of Zoroaster and by the Essenes, a small Jewish group near Palestine.

Each Moslem was commissioned to carry with him a small prayer rug. Wherever he spread it was to become holy ground as, facing Mecca, he repeated the prayer called the *Al-Fatihah* five times each day. Once during his lifetime, if possible, a Moslem was to make a pilgrimage to Mecca.

Some years later after this new faith had become well established, Mohammed carried out his hope to return in triumph to Mecca from which he had been forced to flee.

Declaring, "Truth is come, and falsehood is fled away," he ordered his soldiers to tear down more than 300 idols. This year of 631 A.D. is known in Mohammedanism as the true religion of their fore-

please turn the page

One of the five "pillars" of Islam is the pilgrimage to Mecca (left). Each year since 629 A.D. thousands from all parts of the Moslem world have made the journey.

Traditional forerunners of Islam were the patriarch Abraham (Ibrahim) and his son Ishmael, who are said to have built the original Ka'bah. Within the courtyard of Haram Mosque is this shrine to Abraham, covering a rock which he is said to have addressed the people.

The pilgrims approach Mecca in a sanctified condition, bareheaded, barefooted, and wearing a two-piece, seamless ihram. They make their way to the Haram Mosque, enclosing the holiest structure in Islam, the Ka'bah. Praying, they walk around the shrine seven times.

Having circled the Ka'bah, pilgrims stop to drink at sacred well of Zamzam. Moslems believe the well was revealed by the Archangel Gabriel to Hagar, who, with her son Ishmael, was dying of thirst in the wilderness.

40

41

LIST OF CLASSES

In-person classes were offered in arts, crafts, secretarial skills, speech, photography, English, international relations, government in action and preparation for dynamic maturity.

A SERIES OF RADIO COURSES ADDRESSED THESE TOPICS:

The Enjoyment of Music

Who Am I? (A Psychology Class)

Great Lives After 55

Creative Writing

Everybody's Shakespeare

Adventures in Maturity (Problems in Social Gerontology)

Our American Heritage

Our Place in the Cosmos

How to Get Along With People

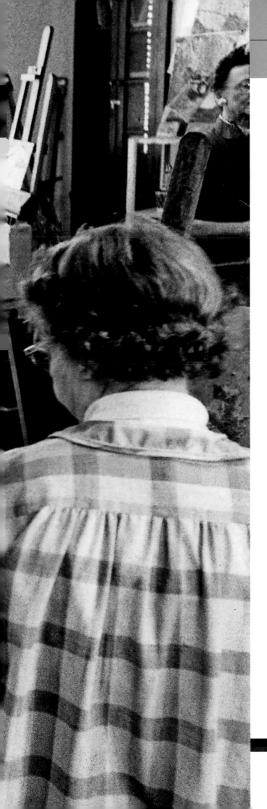

Another inspiration for Dr. Andrus' commitment to lifelong learning was Aldous Huxley, the British novelist and philosopher who, coincidentally, had cofounded Ojai's progressive Happy Valley School. No evidence suggests that Dr. Andrus was present at the school's graduation ceremony in 1951 when Huxley delivered the commencement address, but she later reprinted his address in the *NRTA Journal:*

"In the Prado in Madrid there is a very striking drawing by Goya," Huxley told his audience. "It represents an old, old man, bent double by age and infirmities, tottering along with the help of a staff. Under it is scrawled the caption: Aun Aprendo, 'I am still learning.'"

Dr. Andrus clearly fell into that category, and she hoped to encourage others to follow the same path.

Enrollment in the institute was open to all members interested in developing their skills and abilities. Amid the struggle for civil rights in the United States, the institute "recognizes no barrier of race, color or creed," an introductory article in *Modern Maturity* stated in the August-September 1963 issue. Participants were encouraged to seek out new careers or interests by learning about fine arts, crafts, public speaking, photography, English, music appreciation and international relations—all in preparation for a "dynamic maturity."

Distinguished experts who participated in the "Every Wednesday Morning" lecture series lived the institute's motto: "Age is timeless." A curator from the National Gallery of Art spoke about "Exploring Art: Mental Growth Through Art," for example, and an officer from the Embassy of India described his country's culture.

The Institute of Lifetime Learning was a major success. AARP soon set up a second site, in Long Beach, California, and a third, in St. Petersburg, Florida. Then Dr. Andrus encouraged local AARP chapters to establish their own Lifetime Learning institutes. The San Antonio chapter was the first to take up the challenge, and within a decade 23 of these extension programs ran across the country. Articles in AARP publications shared many of the courses, such as "The World's Great Living Religions and the Part They Play in our Daily Lives," and radio stations were encouraged to broadcast lectures via long-playing albums distributed by the institute.

AARP's Lifetime Learning program was phased out after Elderhostel (now known as Road Scholar) began in the 1970s and after colleges and universities started encouraging adults to attend classes at discounted rates. The AARP program had served its purpose by fostering the idea that learning is timeless.

ART CLASSES SPARKED LATE-LIFE CREATIVITY.

Operations Shift to California

ANDRUS BEGAN SUFFERING serious health problems in the fall of 1963. Her doctors urged her to return to California to recuperate: The pressures of running a national organization from her busy Washington office, they evidently believed, would jeopardize her recovery.

"She was sick in a hospital in New York City when [President John F.] Kennedy died," Ruth Lana recalled. "The doctor said to me, 'She should go and rest. She should go where she wants to be and where she's quiet.' So we came back to California."

Her apartment at Grey Gables in Ojai awaited her. The Acacias was there, too, offering convalescent care. This was the retirement community she had created.

But she didn't return to Ojai. Instead, Dr. Andrus and Lana moved to Long Beach.

Like St. Petersburg, Long Beach was a notable mecca for retirees. That's why AARP had chosen it as the site of its third Hospitality House, with an associated AARP discount pharmacy nearby. This Hospitality House was a family affair. It was run by Lana's sister-in-law, Helen Lana, and it employed Lana's daughter, Lora. Lora's husband, Monty Warren, worked at the pharmacy. Dr. Andrus could thus continue living with friends and family.

Long Beach was also a bigger town than Ojai, and closer to Los Angeles and its international airport, where she could easily hop on a plane to Washington or New York. Dr. Andrus' doctors may have prescribed peace and quiet, but this champion of retirees was not ready to retire. She and Lana merely shifted their base of operations from Washington to an apartment building on Ocean Boulevard in Long Beach.

"Then, as Ethel recuperated and more and more of the work came out here, they rented more and more apartments in that building for offices," Monty Warren recollected. "Everything that she was closely involved with came to Long Beach."

That included the recently founded Institute of Lifetime Learning. The second site was set up in Long Beach not long after Dr. Andrus moved there. Eventually, the headquarters of AARP's field operations moved to Long Beach, along with the editorial offices for *Modern Maturity* and the other publications. The political operation remained in Washington, and the membership office was still based in tiny Ojai, where local AARP employees were swamped early in 1964 by an unexpected event that boosted membership applications into the stratosphere.

The January issue of *Reader's Digest,* then the most widely read magazine in the United States, featured an article about AARP, titled "Dynamic Maturity Is Their

Greetings from LONG BEACH CALIFORNIA

"She was a real team player, and she knew how to get the most out of everybody."

—Monty Warren, western operations manager, talking about Dr. Andrus, shown below in Long Beach

DR. ANDRUS' TRAVEL, 1962

March 7-9:
SAN FRANCISCO
Address regional NRTA-AARP conference

May 27-31:
DENVER
Preside over NRTA-AARP convention

June 24-26:
WASHINGTON, D.C.
Attend regional NRTA-AARP meeting

August 8:
LONG BEACH, CALIFORNIA
Dedicate second Institute of Lifetime Learning site

August 13:
CHAUTAUQUA, NEW YORK
Deliver "Don't Call Me a Senior Citizen" speech

Goal" and subtitled "How an indomitable 79-year-old woman has helped thousands of older persons to achieve meaning and purpose in their lives."

The article noted that AARP's 400-plus paid staff members "regard Dr. Andrus with a mingling of awe and affection, and associates 25 years her junior go breathless keeping up with her as she travels up to 16,000 miles a month, flying to a Senate hearing in Washington, an international conference on aging in Copenhagen, a regional meeting in Salt Lake City. She never lets AARP stop growing."

The article triggered a massive response. Not only did *Reader's Digest* have the highest circulation in the nation, but it was particularly popular with older people.

DESPITE THE HEADLINE in the *Reader's Digest* article, Dr. Andrus was actually 82, not 79, and since falling ill the previous autumn, she was no longer flying thousands of miles a month.

But she still led with vision and vigor. And while her recuperation apparently prevented her from attending the opening of the Dynamic Maturity Pavilion on April 22, 1964, she was engaged in its activities during the two-year fair. Dr. Andrus gloried in the exhibit's success, writing:

"Now, people of all ages from all nations can see and learn of a dramatic new philosophy on aging: Dynamic Maturity! The Pavilion provides a unique showcase for the basic tenets of dynamic maturity—faith in the future; confidence in self; concern for others; and active participation in service."

Her enthusiasm for her pavilion shone through in a 1964 magazine column: "We urge your attendance at our most delightful pavilion whose wonders I must leave to your imagination until you yourself can marvel at its beauty. ... Proudly among this dazzling kaleidoscope of color it sits in its inviting beauty, our testimony of the older folks' continuing value to that society which they themselves have helped create." She reveled in the 450,000 people who had visited the Dynamic Maturity Pavilion during

Dr. Andrus dedicates the Institute of Lifetime Learning in the Times Building (lower right) in Long Beach.

THE INSTITU
OF
LIFETIME LEAR

the fair's two-year run. She also continued to spin off new projects tied to the exhibit's theme, including a new magazine, *Dynamic Maturity*, aimed at preretirees. And she continued to demonstrate, with the arc of her own continuing career, that success was a factor not of age but of commitment and drive. As she said in one of her columns, life is a journey rather than a destination.

But she needed to muster her strength—she would need it in 1965. Congressman Fogarty was planning to reintroduce his Older Americans Act as part of President Lyndon Johnson's ambitious Great Society agenda, much of which awaited congressional approval. At the top of Johnson's legislative wish list was health care protections for older Americans. Its formal title was the Social Security Act Amendments of 1965, but it was better known by a one-word nickname: Medicare.

CHAPTER 8

"AWAKENING TO OUR

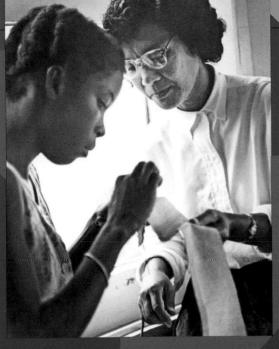

Dr. Andrus encouraged older adults to volunteer through the Peace Corps (shown here) and other service efforts.

Building a greater society

NEEDS"

O**N THE MORNING** of January 24, 1965, Dr. Ethel Percy Andrus was sitting near a window in her Long Beach apartment when she noticed something unusual across the street.

"The flag opposite my window this morning was as usual flying high, whipped by a brisk wind, and then, as I watched, it slowly descended until it rested at half mast," she recalled for her *NRTA Journal* readers in the May-June 1965 issue. "In such a dramatic fashion the world about me learned that the noblest Englishman of the century ... has gone from among us."

Winston Churchill was dead, at the age of 90, and in her article, Dr. Andrus eulogized him with the passion of a longtime admirer. Churchill and Abraham Lincoln were her two foremost heroes, but Churchill's example was especially relevant for her, because he—like she—accomplished his greatest feats after reaching the usual age of retirement. He was a 65-year-old political has-been when his nation finally turned to him for leadership in the dark days of 1940, as Britain struggled to survive against the Nazi blitzkrieg. As prime minister of the United Kingdom, Churchill gave eloquent speeches that rallied the nation. Dr. Andrus owned a record album of those speeches, and she said she would sit and listen to them for inspiration.

"A failure at 65, at 90 the world stands at salute," she wrote. "A great one has gone. We shall not in our lifetime see his like again."

Even Churchill had finally retired from office when he was 80. Dr. Andrus was 83 and still very much at the helm of NRTA and AARP, despite her recent health problems. Her leadership and advocacy skills would soon be tested.

Vital Services

WHEN PURSUING her goals in Washington, Dr. Andrus operated in an intensely political environment. In private, she was in the progressive tradition of President Theodore Roosevelt, but she didn't want AARP to be identified with one party or the other, nor did she want the organization to be seen as a special-interest pressure group, pushing for government handouts for older people.

She stated in a column, "AARP presents in dignified fashion the nonpartisan viewpoint of its membership to Congress and the legislatures of its respective states for their evaluation and action."

Dr. Andrus wanted government to do a better job of supporting and coordinating services that gave retirees the help that they needed to remain in charge of their own lives. That was the point of Congressman John Fogarty's Older Americans Act, which he reintroduced on January 27, 1965.

It aimed to promote development of new or improved programs to help older people secure equal opportunity to an adequate income in retirement, the best possible physical and mental health, suitable housing, opportunity for employment free of age bias, and "retirement in health, honor and dignity." The bill would centralize and energize the federal government's previously piecemeal efforts to help the elderly by creating a U.S. Administration on Aging, directed by a commissioner on aging

appointed by the president and confirmed by the Senate.

In creating this coordinating agency, Fogarty sought to fulfill a major recommendation of the 1961 White House Conference on Aging.

Fogarty was a Democrat, but on retiree issues he worked closely with a Republican, Congressman Melvin Laird of Wisconsin—and they both, in turn, worked closely with Dr. Andrus and AARP Executive Director Bill Fitch.

"Mel Laird became a very good friend of AARP, along with Congressman Fogarty," Fitch recalled.

Fogarty's bill was AARP's No. 1 legislative priority at this time. Fitch, working behind the scenes, helped craft the legislation while Dr. Andrus rallied AARP members to support it. This would become one of the organization's first successful grassroots advocacy campaigns, with members writing letters, sending telegrams and phoning or visiting their senators and representatives. Thanks in part to AARP's efforts, the Older Americans Act enjoyed overwhelming bipartisan support. It passed the House by a vote of 395 to 1, and the Senate by voice vote. A beaming Dr. Andrus watched President Johnson sign the bill into law on July 14, 1965.

"The Older Americans Act clearly affirms our nation's sense of responsibility toward the well-being of all our older citizens," Johnson said. "But even more, the results of this act will help us to expand our opportunities for enriching the lives of all of our citizens in this country, now and in the years to come."

After the ceremony, the president presented Dr. Andrus with one of the signing pens.

SIGNING THE OLDER AMERICANS ACT AFTERWARD, PRESIDENT JOHNSON PRESENTS DR. ANDRUS WITH ONE OF THE SIGNING PENS.

Group Health Care

T HE OLDER AMERICANS ACT was part of Johnson's Great Society agenda. Other laws that cleared Congress during the momentous 1965 session included the measures that comprised the president's war on poverty. Dr. Andrus urged her members to enlist in the campaign, whether as Peace Corps or VISTA volunteers, as foster grandparents or in some other capacity that reflected her enthusiasm for public service.

AARP was also interested in proposals to provide health care coverage to everyone over age 65 and, via Medicaid, to poor people of any age. The need was great: Health costs for older people were rising while their incomes were eroding. And some private insurance companies, other than the one underwriting NRTA and AARP policies, were terminating policies for older Americans in the high-risk category.

Dr. Andrus was well familiar with the challenges of providing affordable health insurance to retired people. By pioneering innovative, affordable group health coverage in 1956, she had demonstrated that companies could insure retirees without losing money. As a result, some assumed Dr. Andrus might be less than enthusiastic about, or even opposed to, the concept of Medicare. Not true. She stated, "[Our association] is proud of the success of our pioneering effort in the cause of health protection, but it wants for all older people the best insurance for the lowest cost."

In 1957 and again in 1959, a health coverage bill for retirees was introduced by Congressman Aime Forand of Rhode Island. The bill was supported by the AFL-CIO and allies of organized labor but opposed by the American Medical Association and many business interests. In hopes of bringing the sides together, Dr. Andrus offered an alternative in 1959, during testimony to the House Ways and Means Committee. AARP believed that its proposal offered broader coverage and addressed the major objections of the medical profession and private industry.

In October 1959, Dr. Andrus used her column in *Modern Maturity* to reinforce the importance of health coverage. "The government awakening to our needs asks what it can supply," she wrote. High on the list was health protection. "Once a luxury, it is now regarded as a necessity in the same category as food, clothing, and shelter. It is the responsibility of society to make available to every older person desiring them the best and the least expensive types of medical protection."

THE RISING COST OF HEALTH CARE

↓

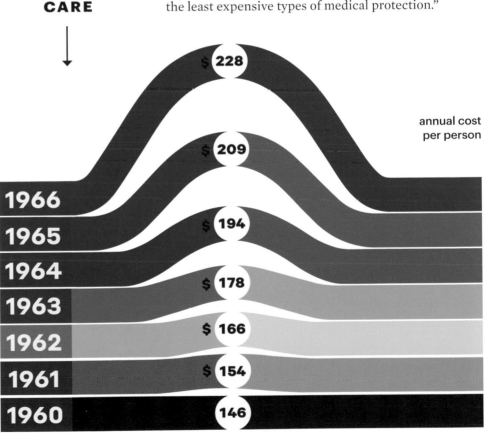

annual cost per person

$ 228

$ 209

$ 194

$ 178

$ 166

$ 154

146

1966
1965
1964
1963
1962
1961
1960

1965 MEDICARE PROVIDED PROTECTION AGAINST THE COST OF HEALTH CARE.

109

The compromise approach Dr. Andrus had proposed was not accepted, and the Forand bill was defeated in two committee votes.

In 1960, Senator John F. Kennedy from Massachusetts made hospital insurance for older Americans—Medicare—a major issue in his presidential campaign. After he was elected president later that year, however, political gridlock stymied progress.

Dr. Andrus testified several times, urging Congress to recognize individuals' freedom of choice and what she called the equality of opportunity. She was concerned that millions of teachers could be forced to pay for Medicare but not be eligible for benefits because they lived in states where Social Security was not granted to retired educators.

"We realize that 4 million oldsters would not be eligible for these benefits, including teachers in states where Social Security is not granted teacher retirees," Dr. Andrus told the House Ways and Means Committee in July 1961. "Our medical goal for the elderly [is] summarized as the need for a medical care program within the reach of retirement incomes, available as a matter of right and not charity."

Working behind the scenes, AARP focused on influencing the Medicare debate to help create a workable compromise. Momentum for action grew in the years following the assassination of President Kennedy, late in 1963.

Although compared with the Older Americans Act, Dr. Andrus had less influence on the final Medicare bill in Congress, it still reflected her ideas.

She had called for a voluntary program; the bill as passed included an optional Part B, for doctor's care and other medical services, which involved a voluntary monthly premium. She had sought Medicare to cover all Americans ages 65 and older, not just those covered by Social Security, and the final bill provided that broader coverage. She had pushed for keeping the Medicare trust fund separate from the Social Security trust fund, and that provision was also in the final bill.

Ethel Says

"Old age is not a defeat but a victory, not a punishment but a privilege."

"I welcome this opportunity to say that our associations are in basic accord with the provisions of this bill, and urge early enactment by the Congress," Fitch testified in May 1965.

The bill passed Congress 10 weeks later and was signed by President Johnson on July 30. "No longer will older Americans be denied the healing miracle of modern medicine," Johnson said in signing Medicare into law. That fall, *Modern Maturity* succinctly summarized the organization's stand on Medicare: "Testified for improvements. Supported final bill."

Soon after, Dr. Andrus began informing members about the new health care program through articles in the *AARP News Bulletin* that described Medicare's provisions and warned members against "swindlers posing as representatives of the Social Security Administration" as Medicare rolled out.

Progress Amid Turbulent Times

JANUARY 8, 1964
President Johnson declares a war on poverty.

AUGUST 7, 1964
With the Gulf of Tonkin Resolution, the U.S. enters the Vietnam War.

NOVEMBER 22, 1963
President Kennedy is assassinated.

JULY 2, 1964
Civil Rights Act becomes law, banning discrimination based on race, color, religion, national origin and gender.

Dr. Martin Luther King Jr.'s nonviolent march from Selma swelled to 25,000 strong.

MARCH 1965
Civil rights marchers are beaten during Bloody Sunday in Selma, Alabama. Two weeks later, Dr. Martin Luther King Jr. leads a nonviolent march to Montgomery. The Voting Rights Act became law in August.

AUGUST 20, 1964
VISTA (Volunteers in Service to America) is created, among other new antipoverty programs.

JULY 30, 1965
Medicare (health insurance for people 65-plus and those with certain disabilities) and Medicaid (health insurance for the poor) are signed into law.

TRUSTED STAFFERS

BILL FITCH
Bill Fitch was appointed the first executive director of NRTA and AARP in November 1959. Dr. Andrus had been impressed with his work as staff director for the upcoming 1961 White House Conference on Aging and, before that, with the Social Security Administration. She insisted that the staff respectfully call him "Mr. Fitch." The motto on his desk read "Vision to see, faith to believe, courage to do."

ERNEST GIDDINGS
Ernie Giddings served as legislative representative of NRTA and AARP from 1961 to 1972, and then served as a consultant until 1986. Previously, he had worked with Dr. Andrus on tax equity for retirees at the National Education Association. For every issue of *Modern Maturity*, he prepared an advocacy update. He said Dr. Andrus' greatest personal qualities included her ability to inspire others, her vision and her "philosophy of helping others grow."

Executive Director Bill Fitch testifies with AARP member Evelyn Garrett on the consumer interests of older Americans before the U.S. Senate.

Expanding Programs

BY SEPTEMBER 8, 1966, when the now biennial AARP convention began its general session in Salt Lake City, the political tussles over Medicare were over and AARP was rolling out its first Medigap plan to supplement and complement the government's new health care program. For Dr. Andrus, two weeks shy of her 85th birthday, this was a moment to savor.

Still only eight years old, AARP was closing in on its millionth member and gaining in stature and influence. Dr. Andrus was mourning her good friend Robert Decormier of New York, who had died a week earlier, but most of the organization's other cofounders were still at her side: Dorothy Crippen, who presided over the opening roll call, and Ruth Lana, Leonard Davis and William Fitch, all of whom addressed the convention. Even Meredith Willson, the musician who had entertained the delegates the previous evening, had a comforting connection with Dr. Andrus: He had composed *The Music Man,* which had made a Broadway star of her old Lincoln High School student Robert Preston.

On the first day of the convention, Dr. Andrus let other people take their turns in the spotlight. The keynote speakers were Congressmen John Fogarty and Melvin Laird, representing both major political parties.

The next morning, Dr. Andrus delivered her "President's Biennium" report. Highlights included the recent purchase of a building in Long Beach to serve as AARP's new western headquarters and distribution of Lifetime Learning classes to radio stations for rebroadcast.

Keeping older drivers safely on the road was another

> "You people are deeply involved. You know what you are doing. You have found wise conclusions."
>
> *–Senator Harrison Williams Jr., chair, Special Committee on Aging*

focus. To showcase positive driver safety efforts, Dr. Andrus presented a citation to Judge Sherman Finesilver of Colorado, who had founded the Denver Driver Improvement School and written about keeping older people safely behind the wheel. Convention delegates also approved a resolution on traffic safety, which pledged "cooperation with responsible agencies in promoting traffic safety and adequate driver education" and recommended that age-based discrimination against older drivers be discontinued. At the time, many drivers—due solely to their age—were charged higher premiums because they were placed in state insurance pools along with reckless drivers and those with repeated motor vehicle violations.

Delegates also learned that AARP was working to make affordable auto insurance available to members. Later named Driverplan 55 Plus, the new insurance plan would be available to members in 1967, along with defensive driving courses offered in cooperation with the National Safety Council.

Promoting driver safety and lifelong learning reflected Dr. Andrus' passion for employing "every iota of imagination, ingenuity, resourcefulness and experience" to create happiness for people as they age.

Once again, Dr. Andrus had identified a widespread problem and addressed it head-on. Her vibrant approach to aging was reflected in her December 1966 *Modern Maturity* column: "AARP is not confined to only those who are retired from a business or profession. Perhaps a better word for the retired in AARP is refired, not retired."

INNOVATIVE PROGRAMS

Clockwise, from top left: Innovative recordings of Institute of Lifetime Learning courses were sent to radio stations in 1966; volunteer tax preparers learn how to help others file taxes in 1975; travelers say "Aloha" as the first NRTA-AARP tour explores Hawaii in 1966; a driver safety instructor teaches one of the courses that sprang from a 1967 AARP-National Safety Council effort.

"DON'T CALL ME A SENIOR CITIZEN"—DR. ANDRUS SPEAKING AT THE CHAUTAUQUA INSTITUTION IN NEW YORK

CHAPTER 9

"TO SERVE, NOT BE

A legacy of lifelong service

THE EXTRA MILE

Ethel Percy Andrus
1884–1967

DR. ETHEL PERCY ANDRUS, A RETIRED EDUCATOR, FOUNDED AARP IN 1958 TO PROMOTE HER PHILOSOPHY OF PRODUCTIVE AGING. SHE INFLUENCED THE MARKETPLACE TO DEVELOP INNOVATIVE SOLUTIONS FOR SOCIAL NEEDS. TODAY, HER ORGANIZATION PROMOTES INDEPENDENCE, DIGNITY AND PURPOSE FOR THOSE AGE 50 AND OLDER, HELPS PEOPLE LIVE THEIR BEST LIVES, AND ENCOURAGES EVERYONE "TO SERVE AND NOT TO BE SERVED."

"What we do, we do for all."

Points of Light Volunteer Pathway

Dr. Andrus was honored with a medallion along the Points of Light Volunteer Pathway in Washington, D.C.

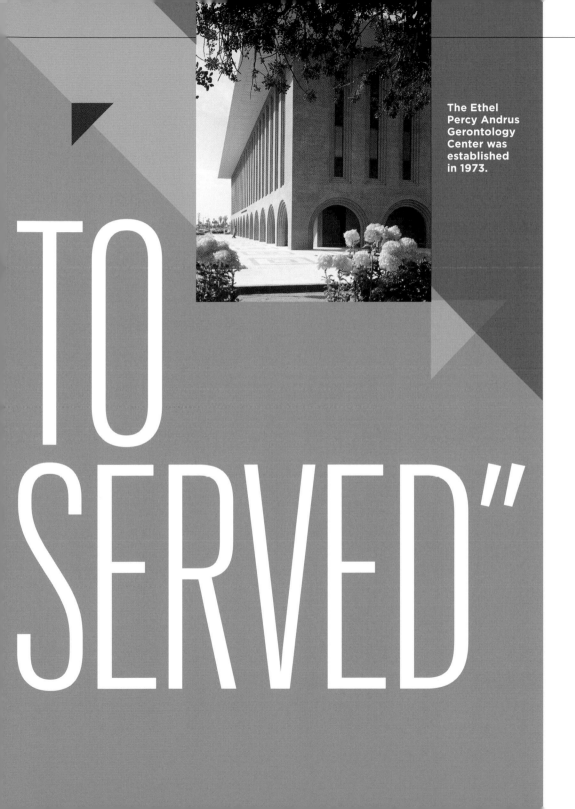

The Ethel Percy Andrus Gerontology Center was established in 1973.

TO SERVED"

1967 and beyond

DR. ETHEL PERCY ANDRUS, if she ever held any doubts on whether her work had made a difference, would have found much to reassure her in the list of proposals to help older people that President Lyndon B. Johnson unveiled in January 1967. His message to Congress mirrored her vision.

"Old age is too often a time of lonely sadness, when it should be a time for service and continued self-development," he told Congress. "For many, later life can offer a second career. It can mean new opportunities for community service. It can be a time to develop new interests, acquire new knowledge, find new ways to use leisure hours. Our goal is not merely to prolong our citizens' lives but to enrich them."

One of Johnson's suggestions must have especially gladdened Dr. Andrus' heart: a bill to outlaw age discrimination in the workplace. Since founding NRTA in 1947, Dr. Andrus had campaigned to end mandatory retirement. Now it seemed that Congress might finally act. (And indeed, the Age Discrimination in Employment Act of 1967 was introduced and signed into law that year.)

The president announced that he was initiating a program "to enlist [retirees] in searching out isolated and incapacitated older people." He also called for increasing Social Security payments so that no retirees would need to live in poverty.

"The talents of elderly Americans must not lie fallow," he wrote. "We should look upon the growing number of older citizens not as a problem or a burden for our democracy, but as an opportunity to enrich their lives and, through them, the lives of all of us."

Loss of a Titan

ON FEBRUARY 6, 1967, the AARP Board of Directors convened in Long Beach. Dr. Andrus presided, as always. But this would turn out to be the last time she held the gavel at one of these sessions. The board amended the bylaws to provide for an orderly transition to new leadership after the organization's founder passed from the scene. Dr. Andrus, now in her 80s, had been experiencing ill health, which was finally forcing her to slow down a bit—although she did so with much reluctance. The great champion of America's retirees had absolutely no interest in retiring before she had to.

On July 9, 1967, she finished her editorial for the October-November issue of *Modern Maturity*. In it, she touched on the wonderful tradition of oral storytelling that preceded the invention of writing.

"Whatever life had taught the oldster in man's continuing battle against evil … whatever life had taught him as techniques to be needed or dangers to be shunned, these lessons he passed on, sometimes in rhyme, often in fable," Dr. Andrus wrote. "Such simple stories, so simply told, so close to the heart of all mankind."

Perhaps she was thinking of the lessons she wanted to

MODERN MATURITY

MEMORIAL
EDITION, JANUARY, 1968

DR. ETHEL PERCY ANDRUS
1884–1967

pass on herself—a summing up of the thoughts she had been sharing, first with her students and then with her AARP and NRTA members in these editorials. Was she formulating some final thought to inspire future generations? We will never know, because that was her last column. Dr. Ethel Percy Andrus died of a massive heart attack four days later, on July 13, 1967, while in the hospital for a routine checkup. She was 85.

IN A SPECIAL MEMORIAL issue published in January 1968, *Modern Maturity* started its tribute to Dr. Andrus by quoting what she had written in the magazine two years earlier when Winston Churchill died: "We have lost a titan."

"We have indeed lost a titan, a woman towering and magnificent in her visions and attainments," the magazine's editors wrote, "a woman with glorious red hair, sparkling eyes, a commanding presence" who "changed reality for millions of Americans in their later years, reshaped the focus of their lives, revived them with

> # "We have indeed lost a titan, a woman towering and magnificent in her visions."
>
> –Modern Maturity
> *Memorial issue*

new hope [and] continuously set world-shaking events in motion."

The first memorial service for Dr. Andrus was held in Washington, on August 23, in the auditorium of the Department of the Interior, a short walk from the White House. Although her friend Congressman John Fogarty had died in January, Congressman Melvin Laird was on hand to pay tribute to her as "a truly great lady and humanitarian."

"The social history of our time will record that when retirement was considered an ending, Dr. Andrus created a feeling of independence, dignity and purpose for the later years," he continued. "At a time when there was no expected role for older persons, Dr. Andrus promoted 'Pride in Participation' as the 1966-1967 conference theme; at a time when the younger generation was being downgraded, Dr. Andrus rose in their defense, expressing her faith in the youth as the strength of our country's future.

"While Dr. Andrus was always a teacher at heart, she was also a most effective communicator. She was an editor's editor, through the beautiful and informative publications of the two associations she founded. It is fitting and deserved that just 10 days before her death, she received an award from the Educational Press Association of America for editorial excellence for her January article in the *NRTA Journal*, entitled 'The Good Samaritan.'

"Dr. Andrus was in every sense that 'Good Samaritan' and will live on as an example of everything she sought to encourage and promote in others. There is no greater tribute or recognition we could pay Dr. Andrus' memory than to say that upon the foundation she built with vision, faith and courage, a better tomorrow has been made possible, for which each of us may reverently add: 'Thank God for sharing Ethel Percy Andrus with us until her task was completed.'"

The other speakers at this service included Leonard Davis, who marveled at how much Dr. Andrus had

President's Message

To members of NRTA:
I would like to share with you a letter, dated July 27th:

"With the passing of our beloved President and Founder, Dr. Ethel Percy Andrus, and in keeping with the by-laws, I have assumed the presidency of NRTA.

"No words can convey the great loss we all feel, nor is it possible to express the debt we all owe to the cherished memory of this great woman whose vision and leadership have made NRTA and AARP a powerful force for good in American life.

"Our first task is to carry on her great work by carrying out the mandates she issued with characteristic foresight before her death.

"But our greater responsibility and objective is to build an ever-stronger and ever-larger organization worthy of her memory, and worthy of her faith in us as heirs to a magnificent tradition.

"Happily, along with the tradition we have inherited a working staff so thoroughly competent, so knowledgeable, and so dedicated to our organization that operations will proceed as smoothly and as efficiently as was her devout wish. As your new Pr....

Cecilia O'Neil

At each Area Conference a preconference leadership meeting was held. The purpose was to call the attention of the Area leaders to their great responsibility and to the important part they play in the activities, programs and policy making. It was evident that more leaders are socially alert and interested in proposed social legislation as it affects all citizens, both young and aging.

Great stress was placed on ...

so profitable and meaningful.
Your President represented each member of NRTA by her attendance at the funeral service of Dr. Andrus. Then she attended the inspiring National In Memoriam held in Washington, D. C., when National leaders in the fields of government, education and aging paid tribute to our Founder President, and later the Memorial Service at Abraham Lincoln High School in Los Angeles, where Dr. Andrus was principal for 28 years. This was a very personal tribute where all participants were either former students or present students at Lincoln High.

Dr. Andrus, master teacher, philosopher and humanitarian, has shown the world how older people might live their retirement years in simple dignity. She has shown how they might share their skills, their understanding and "know how" while serving youth as well as older citizens in their neighborhoods and communities.

To know Dr. Andrus was a privilege, to work with her was an exhilarating ex....

1967
PRESIDENT
LYNDON B.
JOHNSON,
UNABLE TO
ATTEND
ANDRUS'
MEMORIAL
SERVICE,
SENT A
MOVING
TRIBUTE
LETTER.

THE WHITE HOUSE

WASHINGTON

September 25, 1967

The life of each citizen who seeks relentlessly to serve the national good is a most precious asset to this land.   And the loss of such a citizen is a loss shared by every American.

In Ethel Percy Andrus, humanity had a trusted and untiring friend.   She has left us all poorer by her death.   But by her enduring accomplishment, she has enriched not only us, but all succeeding generations of Americans.

Lyndon B. Johnson

been able to accomplish in the 12 years that he knew her. "She experienced setbacks but never knew defeat," Davis said. "The millions of persons, old and young, whose lives have been enriched and will continue to be improved as a result of her vision, will keep her memory bright."

Later that same day, Congressman Laird rose to be recognized in the House of Representatives and asked that the tributes to Dr. Andrus be printed in the *Congressional Record,* including the remarks prepared for the service by Senator Harrison Williams, chair of the Senate Special Committee on Aging, who concluded on this lofty note: "She will be recorded in the history of our time as one of the great women of America."

President Johnson did not attend the service, but he eulogized Dr. Andrus in a letter: "The life of each citizen who seeks relentlessly to serve the national good is a most precious asset to this land. And the loss of such a citizen is a loss shared by every American. In Ethel Percy Andrus, humanity had a trusted and untiring friend. She has left us all poorer by her death. But by her enduring accomplishments, she has enriched not only us, but all succeeding generations of Americans."

Dr. Andrus was laid to rest in Ivy Lawn Memorial Park in Ventura, California, next to her sister, Maud Andrus Service, and Maud's daughter, Ethel Andrus Service, Dr. Andrus' niece and namesake. Twenty miles away in Ojai, her old friends at Grey Gables held their own memorial service for her, on September 1.

"Our service today is dedicated with loving tribute to the founder of Grey Gables, who fused into its foundation and ever-expanding growth the dynamic power and ever-increasing strength of her determination to establish this beautiful Ojai home for retired teachers," said Gables resident Margaret Riggs.

Riggs shared a quotation from Dr. Andrus that had special meaning for her surviving peers, retired teachers now in their 80s who had learned their trade during the Progressive Era from visionary leaders such as Jane Addams and John Dewey. They had founded NRTA

EULOGY

MELVIN LAIRD
U.S. CONGRESSMAN FROM WISCONSIN, WHO LATER SERVED AS SECRETARY OF DEFENSE

"When retirement was considered an ending, Dr. Andrus created a feeling of independence, dignity and purpose for the later years. ... At a time when the younger generation was being downgraded, Dr. Andrus rose in their defense, expressing her faith in the youth as the strength of our country's future."

CLASS OF SERVICE
This is a fast message unless its deferred character is indicated by the proper symbol.
WESTERN UNION
W. P. MARSHALL, CHAIRMAN OF THE BOARD
TELEGRAM
R. W. McFALL, PRESIDENT
SYMBOLS
DL = Day Letter
NL = Night Letter
LT = International Letter Telegram

The filing time shown in the date line on domestic telegrams is LOCAL TIME at point of origin. Time of receipt is LOCAL TIME at point of destination

```
1139P CDT JUL 19 67 MA857 CTA003
M CT WA019 GOV1 NL PD
WASHINGTON DC 19
CECILIA O'NEILL, PRES, NATIONAL RETIRED TEACHERS ASSN
A W SCHLUDEBERG, PRES, AMERICAN ASSN OF RETIRED PERSONS CARE
SHERATON-SCHROEDER HOTEL MILW
ETHEL ANDRUS WAS A GUIDING STAR FOR HAPPY, FULFILLING RETIREMENT
YEARS. WE CAN HONOR HER AS I KNOW SHE WOULD HAVE WISHED BY
EXPANDING SOUND PROGRAMS TO CAPITALIZE TO THE FULLEST ON OUR
ELDERLY CITIZENS' TALENTS, EXPERIENCE AND INTERESTS. THEREBY,
WE WILL BOTH ENRICH THEIR YEARS AND OUR BELOVED NATION WHICH
DOES NEED THEM AS AN INVALUABLE RESOURCE. WE SHALL MISS ETHEL
BUT WE SHALL CONTINUE TO BE INSPIRED BY HER MEMORABLE LEADERSHIP.

        MY BEST WISHES TO YOU, TO YOUR OFFICERS AND MEMBERS.
KINDEST REGARDS                              HUBERT H HUMPHREY.
SF1201(R2-65)
```

CLASS OF SERVICE
This is a fast message unless its deferred character is indicated by the proper symbol.
WESTERN UNION
W. P. MARSHALL, CHAIRMAN OF THE BOARD
TELEGRAM
R. W. McFALL
SYMBOLS
DL = Day Letter
NL = Night Letter
LT = International Letter Telegram

The filing time shown in the date line on domestic telegrams is LOCAL TIME at point of origin. Time of receipt is LOCAL TIME at point of destination

```
LL Q229 (57) CTC453
   CT NA187 PD NEW YORK NY 22 620P EDT        1967   22 PM 7 13
WILLIAM FITCH, CHAIRMAN ETHEL PERCY ANDRUS MEMORIAL COMMITTEE
DEPT OF INTERIOR, DLR 1030PEDT
   AUDITORIUM 18TH AND C STS WASHDC
I'VE ALWAYS BEEN.DISAPPOINTED BECAUSE OUR LODGE AGLOMERATE
MULTI-RACIAL WORLD COULD NOT FUNCTION AS HAPPILY AND AS WELL
AS OUR SMALL AGLOMERATE MULTI-RACIAL HIGH SCHOOL IN LOSANGELES
DID. BUT THEN OUR POOR WORLD HAD NO DR ANDRUS TO RUN IT
   ROBERT PRESTON
   (50)
```

Whereas, The Members of the Senate have been saddened to learn of the death of **Dr. Ethel Percy Andrus,** a pioneer in the development of rights for retired teachers and other retired people; and

Whereas, Dr. Ethel Percy Andrus was born in San Francisco, attended the University of Chicago, and started teaching in 1903, coming in 1911 to Santa M...

TRIBUTE THE CALIFORNIA SENATE HONORED DR. ANDRUS. →

with Dr. Andrus in 1947; they had pioneered Grey Gables with her in 1954; they had been among the first people to join AARP in 1958. They had been rallying to her banner for 20 years, and now she was gone. But she could still inspire them. These are Dr. Andrus' words, which Riggs read aloud:

"Our generation of older folks is a pilot one. How it will be reported by posterity depends on us. We hope we will be judged on our rewarding and interesting lives, and the importance, to ourselves and to society, of our value in personal growth and community participation. We hope we will be judged as having faced confidently an entirely new present and an unknown future, trying to continue in the full stream of life and emphasizing the truth, first, that retirement to us means opportunity; and second, that man does not live by bread alone; that together we can work toward a many-splendored maturity; growing, not just growing old."

Some years had passed since Dr. Andrus had maintained her primary address at Grey Gables, but Ojai attorney Jack Fay—the lawyer whom Dr. Andrus had drafted to file the AARP incorporation papers back in 1958—was still her personal lawyer.

"When Dr. Andrus died in 1967," Fay would later recall, "she had appointed me as executor of her will, and I filed the will for probate in Ventura. ... She was an idealistic visionary, and she was certainly not interested in it for the money. ... And her estate was valued at, as public records in Ventura will show, less than $100,000. It could have been $100 million. But she was not interested in material things."

The third and final memorial service for Dr. Andrus was held at Lincoln High School in Los Angeles, on September 17, 1967, and was attended by more than 1,000 people. The Lincoln Heights community, which she had worked so hard to nurture, had not forgotten her; nor had the teachers who worked under her or the students who attended Lincoln High School during her 28-year

HONOR REPAID

"If we are going to live the years of peace to which this weary world is entitled, and which we passionately want for our children, then we must be strong like Dr. Andrus," Edward W. Brice of the U.S. Department of Health, Education and Welfare said at her memorial service. Almost a year earlier, Dr. Andrus had honored him at an NRTA-AARP convention, for his work in adult and literacy education.

tenure as principal. Many of those former students attended the memorial service.

One who could not attend was Robert Preston, who was starring with Mary Martin in *I Do! I Do!*, a hit play on Broadway that went on to win a Tony Award in 1967. But Preston sent a tribute via telegram:

"I've always been disappointed that our large, agglomerate, multiracial world could not function as happily and as well as our small, agglomerate, multiracial high school in Los Angeles. But then, our poor world had no Dr. Andrus to run it."

In a subsequent letter to Ed Wenig, his former Lincoln High teacher, Preston noted, "The big iron scroll on the [Abraham Lincoln High School] gate through which we passed, seldom looking up, read 'OPPORTUNITY' ... Isn't it amazing that we didn't know until we walked out—OPPORTUNITY HAD RED HAIR."

The color guard paying tribute to Dr. Andrus at her memorial service in Washington

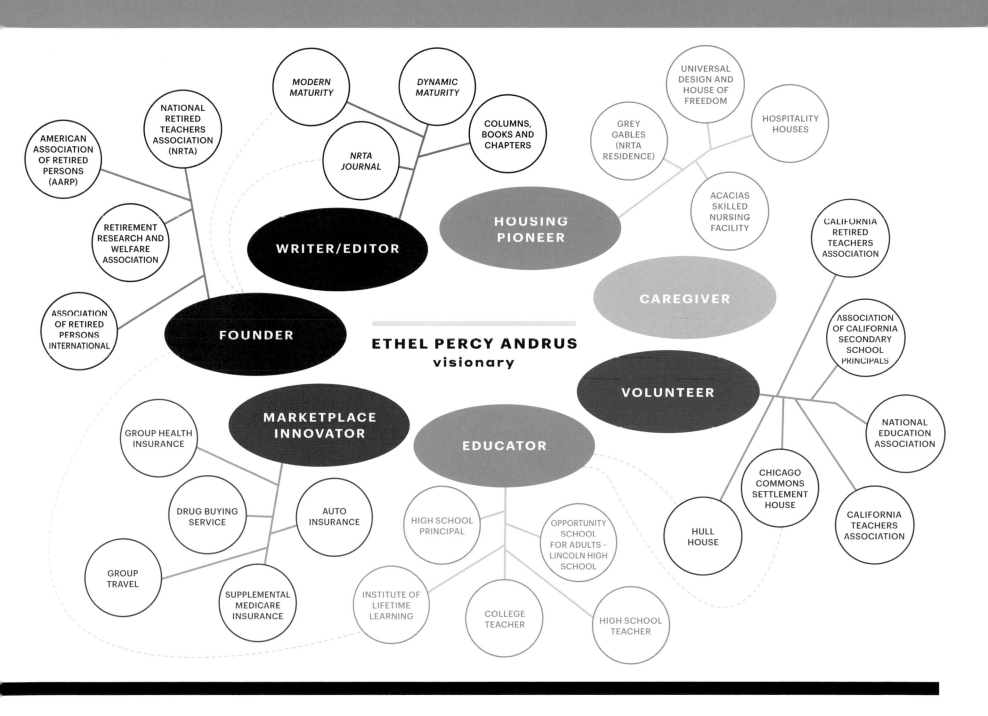

ETHEL PERCY ANDRUS
visionary

WRITER/EDITOR
- MODERN MATURITY
- DYNAMIC MATURITY
- NRTA JOURNAL
- COLUMNS, BOOKS AND CHAPTERS

FOUNDER
- AMERICAN ASSOCIATION OF RETIRED PERSONS (AARP)
- NATIONAL RETIRED TEACHERS ASSOCIATION (NRTA)
- RETIREMENT RESEARCH AND WELFARE ASSOCIATION
- ASSOCIATION OF RETIRED PERSONS INTERNATIONAL

HOUSING PIONEER
- GREY GABLES (NRTA RESIDENCE)
- UNIVERSAL DESIGN AND HOUSE OF FREEDOM
- HOSPITALITY HOUSES
- ACACIAS SKILLED NURSING FACILITY

CAREGIVER

VOLUNTEER
- CALIFORNIA RETIRED TEACHERS ASSOCIATION
- ASSOCIATION OF CALIFORNIA SECONDARY SCHOOL PRINCIPALS
- NATIONAL EDUCATION ASSOCIATION
- CALIFORNIA TEACHERS ASSOCIATION
- CHICAGO COMMONS SETTLEMENT HOUSE
- HULL HOUSE

MARKETPLACE INNOVATOR
- GROUP HEALTH INSURANCE
- DRUG BUYING SERVICE
- AUTO INSURANCE
- GROUP TRAVEL
- SUPPLEMENTAL MEDICARE INSURANCE

EDUCATOR
- HIGH SCHOOL PRINCIPAL
- OPPORTUNITY SCHOOL FOR ADULTS – LINCOLN HIGH SCHOOL
- INSTITUTE OF LIFETIME LEARNING
- COLLEGE TEACHER
- HIGH SCHOOL TEACHER

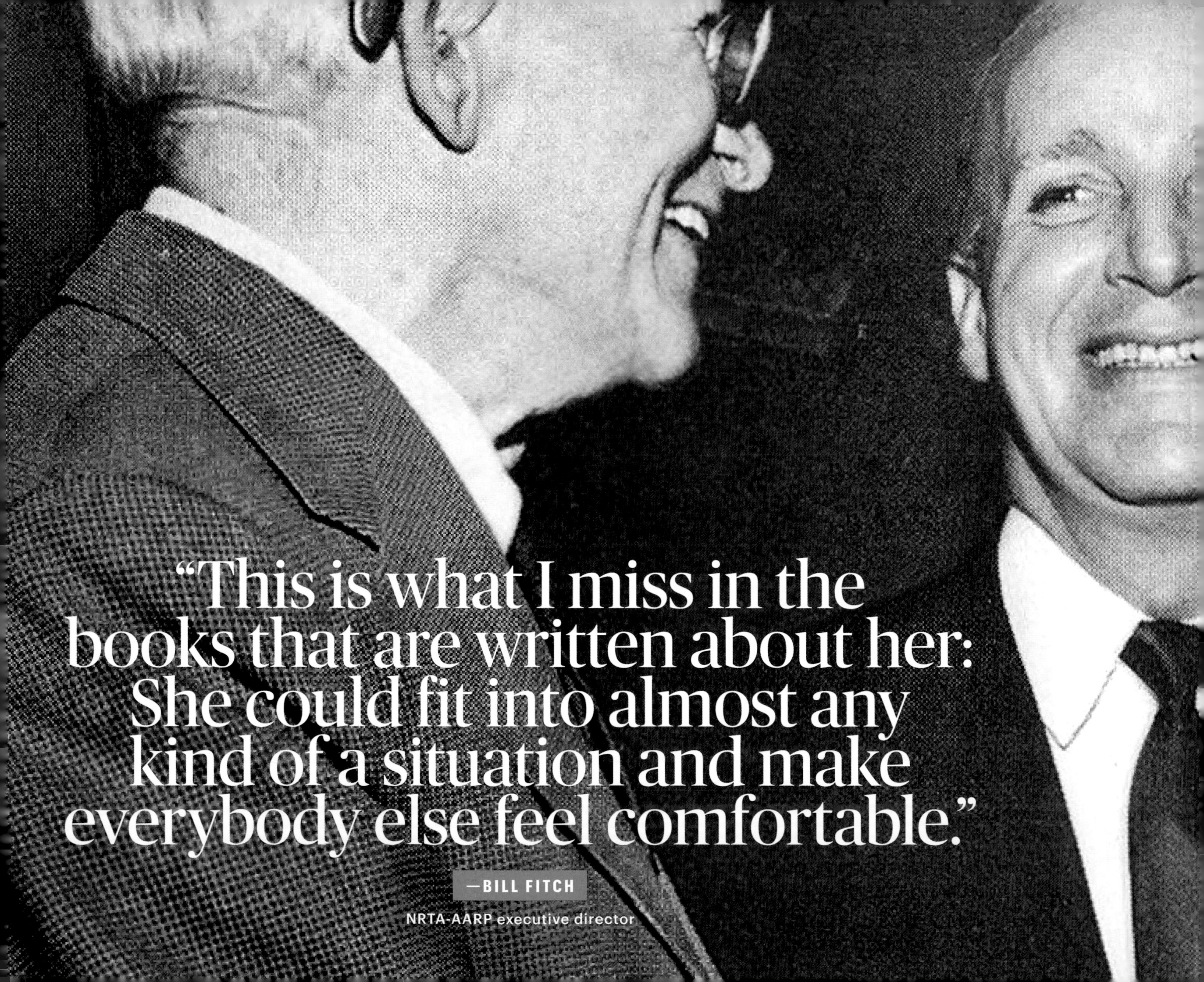

"This is what I miss in the books that are written about her: She could fit into almost any kind of a situation and make everybody else feel comfortable."

—BILL FITCH

NRTA-AARP executive director

DR. ANDRUS WITH
BILL FITCH (CENTER) AND
DAVID McKAY FROM UTAH
1966 NRTA-AARP CONVENTION

The Ethel Percy Andrus Gerontology Center opened in 1973. The Andrus Center is now part of the Leonard Davis School of Gerontology at USC.

Ethel Percy Andrus Gerontology Center, USC

Building a Legacy

S AARP PREPARED to face the post-Andrus era with new leadership, one of the first decisions was how best to memorialize the organization's founder. Dr. Andrus had specifically asked Monty Warren, AARP's western operations manager, that the recently acquired western headquarters building not be renamed for her. Nevertheless, this 12-story tower on Long Beach Boulevard, formerly known as the Times Building, was rechristened the Andrus Building. (AARP no longer owns the property, which its current owners renamed, so Dr. Andrus eventually got her wish.)

In 1968 the AARP board approved a proposal by Dr. Andrus' longtime friend Verna Carley to establish an Ethel Percy Andrus Gerontology Center for the study of aging. AARP approached the University of Southern California, from which Dr. Andrus had earned her master's and doctoral degrees nearly four decades earlier.

As it happens, the approach to USC was well timed. The university had recently hired James Birren, one of the founders of the field of gerontology, to create a new program there. But it lacked adequate facilities. USC agreed to host the new Andrus Gerontology Center, and Birren agreed to run it. The cost to create it would be $4 million—half to come from USC and half from AARP.

The AARP board decided to raise the money itself from among its members—the people who had known Dr. Andrus and who appreciated what she had accomplished. Leonard Davis was named president of the Andrus Memorial Fund. The goal was to raise $2 million in three years. In an early example of crowdfunding, more than 300,000 AARP and NRTA members made contributions. Many were for small amounts—as little as $1.

Others were major bequests. Dr. Andrus' members were eager to honor her memory and to continue her work, and they knew that the proposed gerontology center would serve both purposes beautifully. The contributions poured in, and the campaign exceeded its goal a year ahead of schedule.

"Having been told that we couldn't raise money among older persons, of course we started out with a sense of challenge but with some confidence that the professionals were wrong," remembered Bernie Nash, AARP's executive director from 1969 to 1975. "Sure enough, we raised $2.75 million. So we fulfilled our commitment for the 2 million dollars to USC. And we had this extra $750,000!"

AARP used that spare $750,000 to turn the Andrus Memorial Fund into a new charitable affiliate, the AARP Andrus Foundation, to award research grants in the field of gerontology.

1973
BELOW: RIBBON CUTTING AT THE ANDRUS GERONTOLOGY CENTER. LEFT: DOROTHY CRIPPEN AND RUTH LANA UNVEIL THE PLAQUE.

From left:
Elizabeth Dole,
Colin Powell and
Dorothy Height

Andrus Awards

A HOST OF TRIBUTES honoring Dr. Andrus have helped keep her zest for life and her humanitarian achievements alive.

Chief among them is the AARP Andrus Award, which recognizes individuals who embody AARP's goal of bringing lifetimes of experience to serve all generations.

The first recipient of the Andrus Award, in 1978, was anthropologist Margaret Mead, whom Dr. Andrus had referenced in a *Modern Maturity* column, some 12 years earlier, about cherishing diversity around the world. Dr. Andrus cited Mead's work in helping women complete daily tasks more easily, and in a culturally sensitive way, as an example of an American fostering understanding of other cultures. Other distinguished recipients

> "We are ... pursuing ideas about how to prevent and treat diseases such as Alzheimer's, autism, Parkinson's, epilepsy, schizophrenia."
>
> *—NIH Director Francis S. Collins, winner of the 2008 Andrus Award*

of the Andrus Award have included (pictured above) former U.S. Senator Elizabeth Dole, whose foundation supports the caregivers of military members and veterans; former Secretary of State Colin Powell; and civil rights and women's rights activist Dr. Dorothy Height, former president and chair of the National Council of Negro Women.

In 2008, AARP celebrated its 50th anniversary by paying tribute, throughout the year, to the intergenerational legacy of Dr. Andrus. More than $1 million in awards to high schools nationwide were designed to spark innovation and to foster stronger ties among the generations.

Notably, with a $100,000 Ethel Percy Andrus Legacy Award, the performing arts came to life again at Lincoln High School in Los Angeles—where Dr. Andrus had served as principal for nearly three decades—thanks to

STATE AWARDS

AARP annually presents state Andrus Awards for Community Service, which honor outstanding volunteers who share their experiences, talents and skills to enrich the lives of others in their communities. Recipients in the past have been chosen for their work assisting homeless veterans, mentoring children, providing free tax preparation through AARP Foundation Tax-Aide, supporting the aging LGBTQ community and much more.

the renovation of its rundown theater. Nationwide, community rebuilding efforts, concerts and public forums also promoted "Generations connecting for change."

In 2017, AARP reflected Dr. Andrus' spirit by presenting its first Purpose Prize Awards, to honor people who use their life experience to make a better future for all. One honor, the AARP Andrus Prize for Intergenerational Excellence, recognized work that brings multiple generations together for a better community. In 2017 it honored a retired educator who brings teens and adults together for service-learning trips to communities in need. The other four 2017 awards honored people over 50 who promote girls and science, connect foster children and families with resources, inspire college students to tutor prison inmates and empower young women overseas.

Honoring a Legend

HE NATIONAL WOMEN'S Hall of Fame inducted Dr. Andrus posthumously, in 1993, for her achievements in humanities. Citing her efforts to help older Americans achieve independence, purpose and dignity, the Hall of Fame noted that Dr. Andrus led AARP's rapid growth "by creating an array of programs to help mature Americans with many aspects of their lives, including second careers, health insurance, travel and more."

In 2014 the Ojai Valley Museum mounted a special exhibit titled "Ethel Percy Andrus: How One Woman Changed America." Attendees at the opening reception included Ojai residents who had worked for Dr. Andrus in the AARP membership office before that operation moved to Long Beach; residents of Grey Gables (now called the Gables of Ojai); teachers and students from Lincoln High School; grandchildren of Dr. Andrus' sister, Maud Andrus Service; and Jack Fay, her lawyer. (Ruth Lana's daughter, Lora Warren, attended a preview exhibit at the museum.)

The introductory panel on the exhibit summed up the impact of Dr. Andrus: a patriot, a visionary, an innovator and a great humanitarian:

"Rare is the chicken coop that has an impact on history. But the day Ethel Percy Andrus came upon a retired teacher living in a henhouse, it stirred something deep within her, and launched a chain of events that transformed the lives of millions of Americans. ... Her impact was profound." Dr. Ethel Percy Andrus is one woman who truly changed America. And her legacy endures.

A medallion along the Extra Mile of the Points of Light Volunteer Pathway in Washington—saluting leaders in volunteerism and civic engagement—celebrates the life and service of Dr. Andrus, honored for her "philosophy of productive aging."

"The human contribution is the essential ingredient. It is only in the giving of oneself to others that we truly live."

—*Ethel Percy Andrus*

EPILOGUE

JO ANN JENKINS
CHIEF EXECUTIVE
OFFICER, AARP

AS WE REFLECT on the remarkable story of Dr. Ethel Percy Andrus, we realize that she was many things to many people: a teacher, a patriot, a mentor, a leader, a visionary, a trendsetter, a disruptor, an advocate, an innovator and a voice for older adults struggling to get by. More than anything, she was a catalyst. Our founder believed deeply in the power of individuals to improve their own lives and to lead social change, making life better for others.

AARP has evolved considerably since Dr. Andrus died in 1967. While Dr. Andrus was a visionary, I'm not sure she ever could have envisioned what AARP has become today. It has gone from being a start-up she ran out of her home to one of the most influential and largest nonprofit, nonpartisan organizations in the world. From 1 million members in 1960, AARP has grown to 38 million members, with some 60,000 volunteers; a staff of more than 2,300; and offices in all 50 states, the District of Columbia, Puerto Rico and the U.S. Virgin Islands. And that little magazine she wrote and published from her kitchen table? It's now the most widely read magazine in the United States. Through it all, we have never wavered from the social mission and core values that Dr. Andrus established for the organization in 1958, or her vision of a society in which all people live with dignity and purpose.

I never had the opportunity to meet Dr. Andrus (I was born the year she founded AARP), but I am inspired by her every day, and I consider it an honor to follow in her footsteps. She inspires me to disrupt aging by challenging outdated beliefs and stereotypes; to embrace a culture of innovation; to fight for social justice and end age discrimination, especially in the workplace; and to continue to advocate for and find solutions around the issues she fought for then and we fight for now—health care, financial resilience and personal fulfillment, or health, wealth and self.

As we continue to challenge outdated attitudes and stereotypes, we're helping people recognize the potential benefits of living longer. Because of the issues that Dr. Andrus championed, and that we continue to fight for today, many societies that once looked at the growing aging population and saw only dependent retirees are now beginning to see experienced, accomplished workers. Where they once saw only expensive costs, they're now beginning to see an exploding consumer market that is bolstering our economies. And where they once saw only a growing pool of dependents, they are now beginning to see intergenerational communities with new and different strengths. And it all started because one retired high school principal wanted to help another retired schoolteacher who was living in a chicken coop.

Dr. Andrus would be astounded at how much the world has changed since she started AARP. We live today in a world that is changing constantly and at an increasingly rapid pace. And, as fast as it is changing now, this is the slowest that change will ever be. Just as aging is much different today than it was in Dr. Andrus' time, it will be much different in the years to come. We're approaching a time when people 65 and over worldwide will outnumber children under 5 for the first time in history. Living to 100 is a real possibility, especially for younger generations. A five-generation workforce will be the norm. If we live to 100, many families will have six generations alive at the same time. And our lives will be transformed by autonomous vehicles, the internet of things, virtual reality, augmented reality and artificial intelligence.

As we celebrate AARP's 60th anniversary, I am constantly reminded of how much better people are living and aging today because of the innovations that Dr. Andrus pioneered and the changes she fought for some 60 years ago, and that AARP has continued to champion ever since. As advances in research and technology drive innovation in virtually every field of endeavor that affects our ability to live well as we age, I can't help but wonder what innovations we can create today that people will take for granted 60 years from now because they are living and aging better.

Today, we continue to pursue Dr. Andrus' vision—and our vision—of a society in which all people live with dignity and purpose and where trustworthy information, grassroots advocacy, charitable initiatives, an army of dedicated volunteers, and marketplace products and services continue to be our tools. But we're also designing and experimenting with the tools of our time, such as virtual reality and artificial intelligence, and investing in promising technology. And just as Dr. Andrus reached out to collaborate in her time, we are working with universities, health care systems, banks, entrepreneurs, students, programmers, community leaders and others to find ways of empowering more people to live better as they age.

As we face a future with both enormous opportunity and untold challenges, we will continue to be a strong, powerful and effective advocate, a convener, a global thought leader, an influencer that encourages markets to serve people better, and a voice for multicultural audiences and low-income and vulnerable Americans. In short, we will continue to be all the things Ethel Percy Andrus was.

No doubt Dr. Andrus would be amazed at the world we live in today and by the possibilities the future holds. But I also think she would be very proud, not only of the impact her work has had on millions of people but of AARP's ongoing passion for the work she started decades ago.

Dr. Andrus wrote, "Whatever many may say about the future, it is ours, not only that it may happen to us, but it is in part made by us." As we go about the business of making our future, we will continue to be guided by the vision and values of Dr. Ethel Percy Andrus—one woman who changed America.

Jo Ann Jenkins
Chief Executive Officer, AARP

ACKNOWLEDGMENTS

THIS BOOK would not have been possible without the significant contributions of members of AARP's current and former staff, members of Dr. Andrus' family and allied organizations.

Our author, Craig Walker, of Ojai, California, is a living authority on the life and work of Dr. Andrus, and he was assisted in writing by Mark Lewis, a member of the board of trustees of the Ojai Valley Museum.

Working closely with Craig were a number of dedicated AARP staff colleagues, especially Peggy Laramie and David Albee, who led the historical content and editorial development, and Paul Appeldoorn, whose in-depth knowledge of AARP's organizational history was invaluable.

Art Director Lesley Q. Palmer visually brought to life the story of Dr. Andrus' work and accomplishments, with the help of Jill Foley and Frannie Ruch, who curated a host of photos from various sources. Jodi Lipson, Director of AARP's Book Division, lent her publishing expertise throughout the process. The research team—Lyn Garrity, Angela Johnson and Holly Zimmerman—helped ensure accuracy while copy editors Don Beaulieu, Kim Ferraro, Sharon Hannon, Mary Anne Mulligan and Jennifer Rough helped shape the consistency of the text.

Chris Boardwine managed the workflow and, with Neal Edwards, kept everything on track and production running smoothly. Ed Sikora and Tom Stirling from AARP's Print Center of Excellence coordinated high-resolution scanning and high-quality printing, respectively.

I would be remiss in not thanking the myriad individuals who helped search for documents, retrieve materials from vaults and library shelves, and organize files to make them useful to the author and the historical content team. They include Veralrose Hylton and Charlotte Spinner of the AARP Library; Duane Washington of Records Information Management, assisted by Tom Bayuzik; Kesi Marcus of Employee Communications; CEO Communications Director Boe Workman; and former colleagues Lily Liu, Cal Broughton and Robert Hodder, whose deep historical knowledge and commitment to AARP remain invaluable. Heartfelt thanks go to Barbara and Sandy Service, Dr. Andrus' grandnieces, not only for their assistance with memories and artifacts but also for their ongoing volunteer service through AARP Hawaii. We are also particularly grateful to Lincoln High School for assisting with its historical documents and photos, and to the Parsons Group, owner of the Gables at Ojai, for granting author Craig Walker unfettered access to a treasure trove of Grey Gables' historical documents.

Our hope is that the story of Dr. Ethel Percy Andrus—one woman who changed America—inspires and ignites individual creativity and action across the country and that her legacy lives on in the contributions of a new cohort of caring, action-oriented Americans.

Kevin J. Donnellan
*Executive Vice President and
Chief of Staff, AARP*

"It has been wisely said
that whatever many may say
about the future, it is ours,
not only that it may happen to us,
but it is in part made by us."

—ETHEL PERCY ANDRUS

CREDITS

Cover: Tomasz Usyk
Inside Covers: Kelli Anderson

Table of Contents
Page 2 (lower left), Los Angeles Public Library/Hearst Communications, Inc.
Page 2 (upper center), University Archives and Special Collections, Paul V. Galvin Library, Illinois Institute of Technology
Page 2 (upper right), Retrieved from the Library of Congress
Page 2 (lower right), Alamy
Page 3 (upper left), Jeff Elkins
Page 3 (upper left), AARP
Page 3 (upper center), AARP
Page 3 (upper right), Eli Meir Kaplan
Page 3 (lower right), Keystone-France/Gamma-Keystone via Getty Images

Chapter 1
Page 6 AARP
Page 7 Granger/Granger—All rights reserved
Page 8 Granger/Granger—All rights reserved
Page 9 AARP (2)
Pages 10–11, Smithsonian Institution Archives. Image #MAH-12181
Page 12 (upper left), Stock Montage/Getty Images
Page 12 (right center), North Wind Picture Archives/Alamy Stock Photo
Page 13 (center), Kean Collection/Getty Images
Page 13 (center bottom), Courtesy Special Collections Research Center, Morris Library, Southern Illinois University, Carbondale
Page 14 V.O. Hammon Collection, Newberry Library
Page 15 (upper left), University Archives and Special Collections, Paul V. Galvin Library, Illinois Institute of Technology
Page 15 (upper center), University Archives and Special Collections, Paul V. Galvin Library, Illinois Institute of Technology
Page 15 (lower center), University Archives and Special Collections, Paul V. Galvin Library, Illinois Institute of Technology
Page 15 (lower left), University Archives and Special Collections, Paul V. Galvin Library, Illinois Institute of Technology

Page 16 (lower left), University of Chicago
Page 16–17 AARP
Page 17 (lower right), Bettmann/Getty Images
Page 18 (lower center), Smith Collection/Gado/Getty Images
Page 18 (far right), AARP (2)
Page 19 AARP

Chapter 2
Page 20 (lower left), 1938 Lincolnian, Courtesy Lincoln High School
Page 20 (lower right), 1926 Lincolnian, Courtesy Lincoln High School
Page 21 (upper right), 1926 Lincolnian, Courtesy Lincoln High School
Pages 22–25 Lincolnian Yearbook, Courtesy Lincoln High School
Pages 26–27 1938 Lincolnian, Courtesy Lincoln High School
Page 28 (top center, left), TM & © Walt Disney Productions/Photofest
Page 28 (top center, right), TM & © Walt Disney Productions/Photofest
Page 28–29 (center left), Security Pacific Bank Collection, Los Angeles Public Library
Page 29 (center right), Lincolnian Yearbook, Courtesy Lincoln High School
Page 30, AP Photo
Page 31 (left), Warner Brothers/Getty Images
Page 31 (upper center), California State University, Sacramento. Library. Dept. of Special Collections and University Archives.
Page 31 (upper right), Barbara and Williard Morgan photographs and papers, Library Special Collections, Charles E. Young Research Library, UCLA
Page 31 (lower right), NBCU Photo Bank, Getty Images
Page 32 AARP
Page 33 AARP

Chapter 3
Page 34 AARP
Page 35 (top left), Courtesy The Library of Congress, 379687pu
Page 35 (top left inset), A. Y. Owen/Time Life Pictures/Getty Images
Page 36 Illustration by Alexander Wells

Page 37 AARP
Page 38 (center), twenty1studio/Shutterstock
Page 38 (top right), H. Armstrong Roberts/Retrofile/Getty Images
Page 39 (top left), AARP
Page 39 (bottom left), AARP
Page 39 (top right), AARP
Page 39 (bottom right), AARP
Page 40–41, The Blakelys Photography
Page 42 (top right), SSPL/Getty Images
Page 42 (bottom), AARP
Page 43 Illustration by Matthew Laznicka
Page 44–45 AARP
Page 46 (lower center), Hearst Communications, Inc.
Page 46 (upper center), Los Angeles Public Library
Page 46–47 University of Southern California Libraries

Chapter 4
Page 48 AARP (2)
Page 49 (upper right), StoryBlocks
Page 50 Illustration by Ryan Inzana
Page 51 (top center), Bettmann/Getty Images
Page 51 (center), George Price / The New Yorker Collection/The Cartoon Bank
Page 52 AARP (2)
Page 52–53 AARP
Page 53 (bottom left), Jeff Elkins
Page 53 Family expenses in 1950 source: U.S. Bureau of Labor Statistics, Consumer Expenditure Survey
Page 54–55 SuperStock/Getty Images
Page 56 (upper right), J.R. Eyerman/The LIFE Picture Collection/Getty Images
Page 56 (bottom right), AARP
Page 57 Re-creation from Modern Maturity

Chapter 5
Page 58 AARP
Page 59 (upper left), David Pollack/Corbis via Getty Images
Page 60 (upper left), AARP
Page 60 (upper right), Anterovium/iStock
Page 61 (lower left), Encyclopaedia Britannica Films/Getty Images
Page 61 (top) Illustration by Ryan Inzana

Page 61 (lower middle), Jeff Elkins
Page 61 (center bottom), Jeff Elkins
Page 61 (center right), AARP
Page 62 Jeff Elkins
Page 63 Jeff Elkins
Page 64–65 AARP
Page 66 Illustration by Matthew Laznicka
Page 67 AARP (4)
Page 68 (upper left), AARP
Page 68 Illustration by Steve Sanford
Page 69 (lower left), AARP
Page 69 (lower right), From The New York Times, 1959-06-13 © 1959 The New York Times. All rights reserved. Used by permission and protected by the Copyright Laws of the United States. The printing, copying, redistribution, or retransmission of this Content without express written permission is prohibited.
Page 69 (lower right), STILLFX/istockphoto
Page 70–71 AARP
Page 72–73 AARP
Page 73 AARP
Page 74 AARP (2)
Page 75 (upper center), AARP
Page 75 (lower center), Bettmann/Getty Images

Chapter 6
Page 76 APA-The Engineered Wood Association
Page 77 AARP
Page 79 (upper left), Courtesy the St. Petersburg Museum of History
Page 80, Courtesy Gregory R. Smith (2)
Page 81 (upper left), Housing Authority Collection/Los Angeles Public Library
Page 81 (lower left), © Robert Lautman Photography, National Building Museum
Page 81 (upper right), H. Armstrong Roberts/Retrofile/Getty Images
Page 81 (lower right), The Sun Cities Historical Area Historical Society/Del Webb Sun Cities Museum
Page 82 (lower center), Courtesy Administration for Community Living
Page 82–83, AARP
Page 84 (upper center), illpos/Shutterstock

Page 84 (center right), APA-The Engineered Wood Association
Page 84 (lower right), APA-The Engineered Wood Association
Page 84–85 (far left), APA-The Engineered Wood Association
Page 85 AARP
Page 86 Collection of William Bird
Page 87 twenty1studio/Shutterstock
Page 87 (top left), Andrew Paterson/Alamy Stock Photo
Page 87 (bottom right), AARP
Page 87 (center), AARP

Chapter 7
Page 88 AARP
Page 89 Walter Leporati/Getty Images
Page 90 AARP (2)
Page 90–91 (center), Bill Cotter
Page 92–93 Bill Cotter
Page 94 Illustration by Matthew Laznicka
Page 95 AARP (5)
Page 96 (center left), Bettmann/Getty Images
Page 97 (upper center), Scott Olson/Getty Images
Page 97 (bottom), AARP (2)
Page 98–99 AARP
Page 99 AARP
Page 100–101 AARP
Page 101 (upper center), Found Image Holdings/Corbis via Getty Images
Page 101 (lower right), AARP
Page 102 (upper right), Courtesy Reader's Digest (photo Jeff Elkins)
Page 102 (lower right), Courtesy The Denver Post (photo Jeff Elkins)
Page 103 AARP (2)

Chapter 8
Page 104 AARP (2)
Page 105 (upper right), Paul Conklin/The Granger Collection
Page 106 (top right), Donaldson Collection/Michael Ochs Archives/Getty Images
Page 106–107 (right), LBJ Library Photo by WHPO photographer
Page 107 (lower right), LBJ Library Photo by Yoichi Okamoto
Page 108 Social Security History Archive & Museum
Page 109 Rising cost of health care source: Kimberly Amadeo, U.S. economy expert for TheBalance.com
Page 110 (lower left), Bettmann/Getty Images

Page 110 (lower right), National Archives/111-CC-73170
Page 111 (lower center), Courtesy CNCS
Page 111 (upper left), Bettmann/Getty Images
Page 111 (right), AARP (2)
Page 112 AARP
Page 113 (lower center), Bettmann/Getty Images
Page 114 AARP (4)
Page 115 AARP

Chapter 9
Page 116 Eli Meir Kaplan
Page 117 AARP
Page 118 Jeff Elkins
Page 119 Jeff Elkins
Page 120 AARP
Page 121 (center), Afro American Newspapers/Gado/Getty Images
Page 121 (right), AARP (3)
Page 122 AARP (2)
Page 124–125 AARP
Page 126 Smith Collection/Gado/Getty Images
Page 127, AARP (2)
Page 128 (upper left), Keren Carrion/The Hill
Page 128 (bottom left), Jeff Elkins
Page 128 (top center), Paul J. Richards/AFP/Getty Images
Page 129 (top right), NY Daily News Archive via Getty Images
Page 130 Eli Meir Kaplan
Page 131 Illustration by Martin Sati

Epilogue
Page 132 Illustration by Tomasz Usyk

Photo colorizations:
Sanna Dullaway, pages 16 (center), 22, 40, 54, 68 (left), 72, 84 (center spread), 98, 112

Infographics: Kelli Anderson, pages 53, 78, 79, 102, 109, 123

Photo enhancements:
Chris O'Riley, pages 9 (left), 15 (bottom left), 18 (bottom), 29 (right), 33, 46 (bottom), 47 (left), 62 (left), 63, 67 (bottom), 69 (bottom right), 74 (bottom), 86, 95 (top right, center left), 97 (bottom), 100, 108, 126

Chapter opener patterns:
Kelli Anderson

"Ethel Says" illustration:
Kyle Hilton

Art Director: Lesley Q. Palmer | Creative Director: Scott A. Davis | Director of Photography: Michael Wichita